In *The Collapse and Recovery of the Roman Empire*, Michael Grant asserts that the fact that the Roman Empire of the third century AD did not collapse is one of the miracles of history. He argues that at that time the Empire seemed ripe for disintegration and he expresses amazement that it continued, in the west, for another two hundred years and, in the east, for far longer. Michael Grant examines the reasons for the collapse of the third-century Roman Empire, (including analyses of the succession of emperors, the Germans and the Persians) and conversely, the reasons for its recovery, including discussions of strong emperors, a reconstituted army, finance and coinage and state religion.

The Collapse and Recovery of the Roman Empire presents a study of third-century Rome, which is a lavishly illustrated and lucid read, typical of Michael Grant's inimitable style and learning.

THE COLLAPSE AND RECOVERY OF THE ROMAN EMPIRE

THE COLLAPSE AND RECOVERY OF THE ROMAN EMPIRE

Michael Grant

London and New York

First published 1999
by Routledge
11 New Fetter Lane, London EC4P 4EE

Simultaneously published in the USA and Canada
by Routledge
29 West 35th Street, New York, NY 10001

Typeset in Garamond by
J&L Composition Ltd, Filey, North Yorkshire
Printed and bound in Great Britain by
Butler and Tanner Ltd, Frome and London

British Library Cataloguing in Publication Data
A catalogue record for this book is available from the British Library

Library of Congress Cataloging in Publication Data
Grant, Michael, 1914–
Collapse and recovery of the Roman Empire/Michael Grant.
p. cm.
Includes bibliographical references and index.
1. Rome–History–Period of military anarchy, 235–284.
2. Emperors–Rome–Biography. 3. Rome–History–Empire, 284–476.
4. Byzantine Empire–History–To 527. I. Title.
DG305.G73 1999
937′.06–dc21 98-8222
CIP

ISBN 0–415–17323–X

CONTENTS

CONTENTS

ILLUSTRATIONS

FIGURES

ILLUSTRATIONS

MAPS

LIST OF EMPERORS

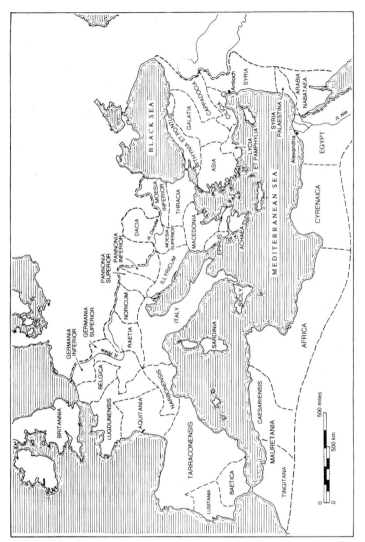

Map 1 The Roman provinces

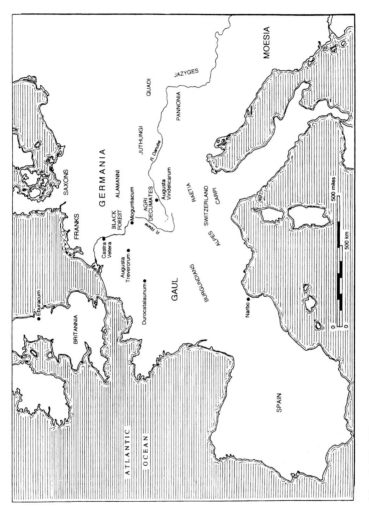

Map 2 The West

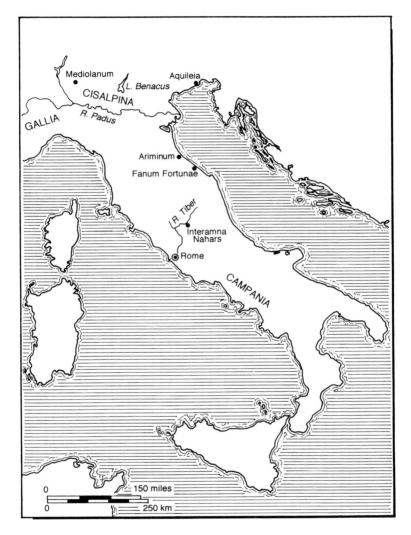

Mediolanum
CISALPINA
L. Benacus
Aquileia
GALLIA
R. Padus
Ariminum
Fanum Fortunae
R. Tiber
Interamna
Nahars
Rome
CAMPANIA

0   150 miles
0   250 km

Map 3 Italy

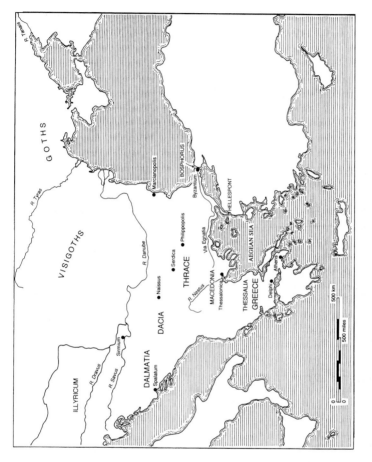

Map 4 The Balkans

Map 5 Asia Minor

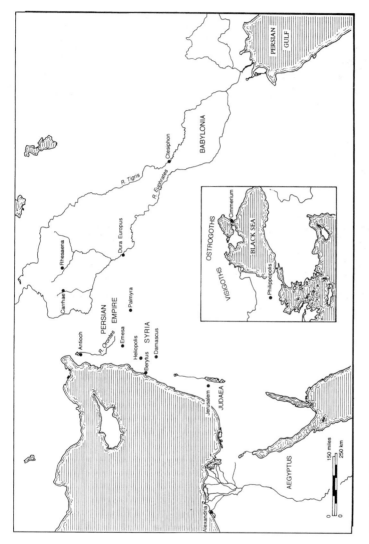

Map 6 The East

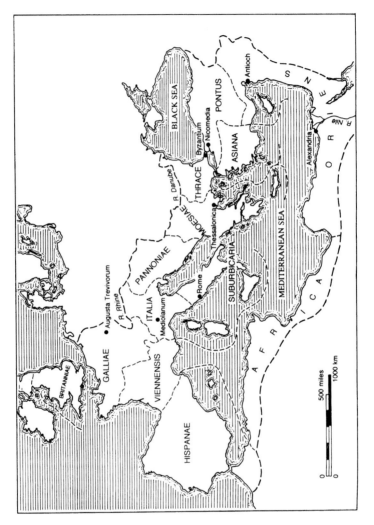

Map 7 The administrative dioceses of Diocletian

INTRODUCTION

The interesting thing about this period is that the Roman empire – of which the past history, together with that of the Greeks which is inherited, is summarily added in an Appendix – showed every sign of collapse. But it did not collapse – it went on, in the west, for another two hundred years, and in the east for far, far longer. Why and how was this? I have never seen this issue frankly and adequately discussed. Certainly, any number of people have written about the third century and its personalities, and in this book I have not been afraid to quote from them. Indeed, I have done so to such an extent that I may be held guilty, I am aware, of patch-work or *pastiche*. But I have done so on purpose, because in my view it would be too egotistical to suppose that no one had written about the period at all, or to any purpose. However, I have tried not to lose sight of the main feature of the epoch, which is, I have said, that the Roman empire seemed ripe for complete disintegration, but that this did not occur.

Even if this volume does quote scholarly writers, it is not particularly, or essentially, scholarly: what I have sought in it is to bring home what really happened. Nor is the present book unduly sympathetic to the Roman empire; the Germans and Sarmatians and Persians also had something to be said for them. Yet it was the Roman empire which is a sort of precursor of the united Europe which many of us would like to see in existence today: see also the Epilogue.

The fact that the Roman empire did not collapse in the 260s or 270s AD is one of the miracles of history,[1] and shows how careful we ought to be in asserting what will happen, or ought to happen. To historiographers it is an uncomfortable fact but an inescapable one. For one thing, as has already been said, the empire did not collapse, but recovered. When it recovered, it was by no means the same as it had been before; but surely that was only to be expected. What happened to it, in other words, why it was not the same as it had been before, is part of this story. Another part concerns the writers to whom those who were disgusted by the whole depressing military and political situation had recourse, and they included a great philosopher, Plotinus, and an unforgettable novelist, Heliodorus.

I am grateful to the following publishers, from whose publications I have quoted: where necessary I have obtained permission to do so: Blackwell Publishers (Todd, *The Early Germans*, 1992); British Museum Publications Ltd., copyright Trustees of the British Museum (R.A.G. Carson, *Principal Coins of the Romans*, vol. III, 1981); Cambridge University Press (*Cambridge Ancient History*, vol. XII, 1956; P.E. Easterling and B.M.W. Knox (eds.) *Cambridge History of Classical Literature I*, 1985; M. Grant, *Roman Literature*, 1954; M. Grant, *Roman History from Coins*, 1958; *Encyclopaedia Britannica* Inc; (1971 ed.) (E. Strong, *Art in Ancient Rome*, 1929); Hutchinson (D.R. Dudley, *The Romans*, 1970); Oxford University Press (*Oxford Classical Dictionary*, vol. II, 1970, vol. III, 1996); Penguin (A. Boethius and J.B. Ward-Perkins, *Etruscan and Roman Architecture, 1971*); Phaidon (M.R. Scherer, *Marvels of Ancient Rome*, 1956); Routledge (N. Holzberg, *The Ancient Novel*, 1995; M. Grant, *Art in the Roman Empire*, 1993); Scribners (M. Grant, *Readings in the Classical Historians*, 1992); Thames and Hudson (J.M.C. Toynbee in L. Rossi, *Trajan's Column and the Dacian Wars*, 1971); Weidenfield and Nicholson, Orion Publishing Co. (M. Grant, *The Emperor Constantine*, 1993). I also owe special thanks to Richard Stoneman, Coco Stevenson and Sarah Brown of Routledge and to Susan Dunsmore.

Part I

COLLAPSE

1

THE SUCCESSION OF EMPERORS

One of the main problems with the Roman empire was its incessant changes of emperor. The succession to the throne had never been effectively worked out, but now things were much worse, since the army often proceeded to kill the reigning emperor (see Figures 1 and 2) and appoint his successor, who was also killed not very long afterwards.[1]

> Typical of this situation, in many ways, was the frightening emperor Maximinus I (235–238). Julius Verus Maximinus, Gaius, also known as Maximinus Thrax ('the Thracian'), a Danubian of relatively humble stock, exploited the opportunities of the Severan army to gain numerous senior appointments. He became emperor by chance at Mainz (Moguntiacum, March 235) in the mutiny against . . . Severus Alexander.
>
> An equestrian outside the ruling clique, he was unsure of his position. He attempted to conciliate the senate from afar, remaining on the frontier with his troops and attempting to act the successful warrior–emperor; he campaigned vigorously over the Rhine and Danube. However, his overtures were unwelcome, his absence from Rome politically unwise, and his wars expensive. The revolt of Gordian I recalled him to Italy, where he then faced Balbinus and Pupienus. The stubborn resistance of Aquileia caused Maximinus to lose his judgment, and the military initiative. His troops became disheartened with the lack of progress and finally murdered him and his son (spring 238).[2]

Here is more about Gordian I, who unsuccessfully revolted against Maximinus I.

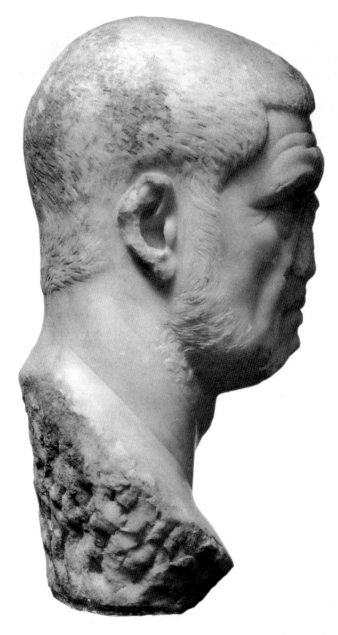

Figure 1 Bust of Maximinus I Thrax (235–8) (Ny Carlsberg Glyptotek, Denmark).

Figure 2 Coin of Pupienus. (Photograph courtesy of Michael Grant)

Gordian I (Marcus Antonius Sempronius Romanus), Roman emperor AD 238. An elderly proconsul of Africa, he intervened in a plot against Maximinus I, only to find himself proclaimed emperor. He made his son, Gordian II, his colleague. The senate, also hostile to Maximinus, quickly acknowledged them.

However, the rebels were militarily weak, and when Capel[l]ianus, governor of Numidia, moved against them with his legionary army, Gordian II was killed and Gordian I committed suicide, after a reign of only a few weeks (early 238).[3] The senate, compromised, continued the insurrection under Balbinus and Pupienus.

Balbinus (Decius Caelius Calvinus) and Pupienus (Marcus Clodius Maximus), members of a board of twenty *consulares* appointed by the senate for the defence of Italy against the emperor Maximinus, were after the deaths of Gordian I and II chosen joint emperors by the senate (AD 238). Both had had long senatorial careers. Constitutionally, on the model of the consulate, they had equal powers, each being *pontifex maximus*, but Balbinus was entrusted with the civil administration and Pupienus with the command of the army. To placate the people, the boy Gordian III was given the status of Caesar. At the news of Maximinus's murder Pupienus proceeded to Aquileia and sent back the former's legions to their provinces, and with his bodyguard returned to Rome to share a Triumph with Balbinus and Gordian.

For a few days the government worked smoothly, but the praetorians, who resented the senate's action, mutinied. The two emperors were dragged from their palace and murdered after reigning for three months.[4]

Gordian III was their successor (see Figure 3), but he was very young, the conduct of affairs being for the most part in the hands of Timesitheus, whose subsequent death laid the empire wide open. But Gordian III, unlike almost every other emperor of the

Figure 3 Bust of Gordian III (238–44) (Museo delle Terme, Rome. Archivi Alinari/Anderson).

period, was not murdered but died (at Zaitha), perhaps of wounds. His rulership had been largely ineffective. Here is a more detailed account of his reign:

> Gordian III (Marcus Antonius Gordianus), grandson of Gordian I by a daughter, was forced on Balbinus and Pupienus as their Caesar and after their murder (mid-AD 238) saluted emperor by the praetorians at the age of 13.
>
> The conduct of affairs was at first in the hands of his backers but, as fiscal and military difficulties increased, it passed to the praetorian prefect Gaius Furius Sabinius Aquila Timesitheus (241). Timesitheus prepared a major campaign against Persia which, beginning in 242, achieved substantial success before his death, by illness, in 243. Gordian replaced Timesitheus with one of the latter's protégés, Marcus Julius Philippus, who continued the war. However, the Roman army suffered defeat near Ctesiphon [Kut], and shortly afterwards Gordian died (early 244). He was succeeded by Philippus.
>
> Though the period of the Gordians shows some of the characteristics of the third-century 'crisis', it is best interpreted as a reversion to the Severan monarchy after the aberrance of Maximinus.[5]

Philip, his successor, was not a Roman or Italian. Here are some further particulars about him (see Figure 4).

> Philip (Marcus Julius Philippus), Roman emperor AD 244–9. An Arabian from Shahba (SE of Damascus), he became praetorian prefect of Gordian III and, early in 244, succeeded him as emperor.
>
> After making peace with Persia, he immediately went to Rome. His reign saw the thousandth anniversary of the city (247–8), and the beginning of the third century 'crisis' proper, characterised by invasion over the Danube and Roman civil war. Philippus repelled the Carpi (245–7), but left Pacatian's rebellion . . . to Decius (248–9). Decius' troops proclaimed him emperor in summer 249, and in the autumn he defeated and killed Philippus at Verona.[6]

Philip had ruled for five years, but his reign had been neither peaceful nor useful. No better was that of his successor Decius (see Figure 5), whose emperorship lasted for two years.

Figure 4 Bust of Philip (244–9) (Museo Vaticano, Rome. Archivi Alinari/ Anderson).

Decius (Gaius Messius Quintus), emperor 249–251, born in Pannonia, but of an old senatorial family, had already achieved high office before being appointed by Philip to restore order on the Danube. His success, and Philip's unpopularity, caused his troops to declare him emperor and compel them to overthrow his patron.

In 250 the Carpi invaded Dacia, the Goths, under Kniva, Moesia. Decius was defeated near Beroea [Verria]. The following year, in an attempt to intercept the Goths on

8

Figure 5 Bust of Decius (249–51) (Museo Capitolino, Rome. Archivi Alinari/Anderson).

their way home, he and his son Herennius [Etruscus] were defeated and killed at Abrittus [near Razgrad].

Decius was a staunch upholder of the old Roman traditions. His assumption of the additional surname of Trajan promised an aggressive frontier policy, and his persecution of Christians resulted from his belief that the restoration of state cults was essential to the preservation of the empire

9

. . . However, his approach was outdated, and his reign initiated the worst period of the third century 'crisis'.[7]

Decius's death at Abrittus, at the hand of the Goths, was a unique feature, as this was the one and only occasion when a Roman emperor was slain by an enemy. It marked a very low point in the history of the Roman empire. The successor of the slain emperor was Trebonianus Gallus (see Figure 6).

> Trebonianus Gallus (Gaius Vibius) ruled AD 251–3. A successful senatorial governor of Moesia, he was acclaimed by the army immediately after Decius' death.
>
> He made an unfavourable peace with the Goths, then returned to Rome, where he adopted Decius' young son [his second, Hostilianus]. . . . Perhaps distracted by the effects of a severe plague, he appeared to ignore renewed Persian aggression (including the capture of Antioch), and failed even to return to the Danube to avenge his predecessor (whose end he was suspected of having contrived). When the Danubian troops forced Aemilian's usurpation in 253 (early summer), Gallus sent Valerian to gather reinforcements, but he was killed at Interamna Nahars [Terni] by his own men before these could arrive (late summer).[8]

Figure 6 Medallion of Trebonianus Gallus. (Photograph courtesy of Michael Grant).

The reign of Trebonianus Gallus was a period of unmitigated disaster, accentuated by plague and famine. One can now see the imperial rulership at its worst: in the hands of a soldier, who proved inadequate and unsuccessful. Of his short-lived successor Aemilian (see Figure 7), the following has been said:

> Aemilian (Aemilius Aemilianus, Marcus), emperor AD 253. Against imperial policy, while governor of Moesia, he dealt harshly with the Goths, and was proclaimed emperor by the army.
>
> He marched on Italy, overthrew Trebonianus Gallus, but was soon killed by his own troops, panicked by the approach of Valerian. The civil strife of 253 exposed Greece to Gothic invasion.[9]

Aemilian had only lasted a very short time. He was typical of the military men who now, without much success, aspired to rule the empire. His successor was Valerian (see Figure 8), who reigned much longer, but came to a disastrous end:

> Valerian (Publius Licinius Valerianus), ruled AD 253–60. An elderly (in his 60s) noble senator of great experience, he was sent to Raetia to gather troops to help Trebonianus Gallus against Aemilius Aemilianus. On the death of Gallus, he was hailed as emperor by his men, and marched on Italy. Following the murder of Aemilianus, Valerian and his adult

Figure 7 Coin of Aemilian. (Photograph courtesy of Michael Grant).

son Gallienus were universally recognised as Augusti. Both strove to serve the empire in circumstances that, as growing external pressures exacerbated internal economic, political and moral weaknesses, were becoming ever more difficult.

However, their joint reign saw the nadir of the third century 'crisis'. In 254 Valerian moved east to repair the damage done by the Persians under Gallus and Aemilianus, and to repel new Gothic raids (in 253/4. 254/5, 256) down the eastern and western coasts of the Black Sea into Asia Minor. The strain he was under is reflected in his persecution of Christianity (rescripts of 257, 258) and his increased reliance on Septimius Odaenathus of Palmyra [Tadmor]. It was perhaps the need for peace which tempted him to negotiate personally with Sapor I when the latter again invaded the empire in strength, and which led to his capture, with most of his general staff (summer 260). Valerian was subjected to various humiliations, and died a prisoner.

In outlook remarkably similar to Decius, Valerian may be seen as the last of the senatorial warrior–emperors, who had pursued a combined civilian and military career. . . . As Gallienus recognised, new problems demanded new solutions.[10]

Figure 8 Coin of Valerian (253–60). (Photograph courtesy of Michael Grant.)

Despite a great deal of vainglory on the imperial coinage, Valerian's reign marked unparalleled catastrophes, culminating in the imprisonment of the emperor himself by his enemy, the only occasion on which this occurred.

There were a great many usurpers of the imperial role at this period.[11] That, in itself, is a testimonial to the weakness of the imperial position and indeed of the empire. The army continually declared its commanding officers emperors. Most of them did not last very long, and do not deserve a great deal of attention, because they had little influence on the development of events – except that their usurpations encouraged the peoples across the frontiers to invade. But Odaenathus is an exception. He ruled at Palmyra,[12] and in truth governed the whole of the Roman east, but he is unusual because he continued to recognise the authority of the emperor at Rome. He resisted the Persians, and thereby performed a very valuable service. He was also useful because he continued, as has already been said, to recognise the emperor Gallienus at Rome (see Figures 9 and 10), as most of the usurpers did not.[13]

Odaenathus (Septimius) was a Palmyrene noble[14] who from c.250 cleverly exploited the weaknesses of Rome and Persia to establish his city, with himself as its king[15] as a major power in the east. He was already a valued ally under Valerian,[16] and Gallienus acknowledged his loyalty.

> The relation of Odaenathus to Gallienus is precisely defined by the titles which the Palmyrene prince received from his overlord. On his first expedition against Persia he had already at his disposal the remains of the Roman army; he must have held the title of *dux Romanorum*. This is an exceptional position, in which the exact powers are deliberately left undefined, as is likewise the case with the civil title of this prince. . . . The civil and financial administration was [not] allotted to him, [though] he enjoyed a certain right of supervision.
>
> Apart from the Roman titles of honour, the dignity of the Palmyrene ruler is now described by the new title 'King of Kings'. . . . The name did emphasise . . . a rivalry with the Great King of Persia. . . . The position of the mighty sheikh fell little short of imperial autocracy. . . . Odaenathus, indeed, was originally no convinced adherent of Rome. . . . It appears as if the second victory over Persia widened

Figure 9 Bust of Gallienus (Museo delle Terme, Rome. Archivi Alinari/ Anderson).

Figure 10 Coin of Gallienus. (Photograph courtesy of Michael Grant).

the horizon of his ambition and as if he was meditating a breach with Rome.[17]

Zenobia or in Aramaic Bath Zabbai, was one of the great women of classical antiquity. The second wife of Septimius Odaenathus of Palmyra, on his death in AD 267, she secured power for herself in the name of her young son, Septimius Vaballathus.[18]

She was perhaps responsible for the murder of her husband and her son by a previous marriage; at any rate she thereupon secured the power for herself in the name of Vaballathus. Gallienus sent Heraclianus against her, but he was defeated, and Zenobia, having secured Syria and devastated Bostra (Bosra) in AD 269 (or a little later), conquered Egypt, and in *c.*270 overran most of Asia Minor.[19]

2

THE GERMANS[1]

By far the most serious threat to the Roman empire came from the frontiers, where the people who lived there, egged on by the constant changes – and consequent weakness – in the imperial authority, were in a constant state of revolt. In the north of the empire, especially, the frontier virtually ceased to exist, over a prolonged period.

> In earlier studies of Roman–barbarian relations two opposing points of view can be distinguished. One group of scholars . . . emphasises trade as the main reason for the influx of Roman imports. The other group . . . take account particularly of political acts such as paying tribute, taking booty and giving and receiving of gifts.[2]

Relations had to some extent changed. That is to say, there were now numerous Germans in the Roman army; and the Germans, or some of them, had tended to adopt certain features of Roman life.

Yet there were three main areas where the 'free' Germans seemed determined to break through the Rhine–Danube frontier.[3] The first was on the Rhine, the second on the Upper Danube, and the third was at the mouth of the Danube. In the first and, to some extent also, the second area the principal opponents were the Alamanni (Allemanni, 'all of them'), of whom the following has been said:

> [They were] a Germanic people forming a loose confederation of tribes in western Germany in the third and later centuries AD. . . . Their raids on the Roman provinces became serious from the 250s. In the fourth century they exploited Roman abandonment of the Agri Decumates to

16

settle south of the River Main [Moenus]. They frequently
harrassed Gaul, but their chief danger to the empire lay in
their ability to invade Italy from over the Alps. . . .

The diffusion of political power (among many kings and
princes) ensured that, though often defeated in battle, the
Alamanni could never be broken by Rome.[4]

The second area in which the Germans threatened the empire
was the central zone in which Italy itself came under threat through
the province of Raetia.

Raetia was a Roman province including Tyrol and parts of
Bavaria and Switzerland. Although small, Raetia was important
because it blocked potential invasion-routes and Italy. During the
troubles of the third century, when, now lacking the protection of
the trans-Danubian *limes* and the Agri Decumates which were
totally lost in *c*.260 or 263, Raetia faced barbarian invaders and
Gallic usurpers alike. The frontier, such as it was, was rolled back,
and the Alamanni settled there.[5]

But the most serious menace of all came from the Goths, at the
mouth of the Black Sea.

The first detachments [of Goths] arrived in the Black Sea
area about 170 and settled between the Don and the
Dniester [Tyras]. More groups arrived between 200 and
230. In 257 there took place a series of raids, partly for
booty and partly in the search for land, into the territories of
the eastern Roman empire. They also occupied the Roman
province of Dacia, roughly modern Roumania. This
indicates an extensive western expansion from the Dniester
along the western shores of the Black Sea and westward
north of the Danube river.

By 260 the Goths had split into two groups: the
Ostrogoths (East Goths) and the Visigoths (West Goths).
The reason for the division is not known . . . In 264 there
was a Gothic landing at Trebizond [Trabzon], and a raid
through Cappadocia, Galatia and Bithynia.[6]

The first certain indication of a rising barbarian power
north of the Danube had come in 238, when an army of
Goths broke across the Danube close to its mouth and
pillaged the Roman province of Lower Moesia. They
extracted payment from the Roman government before
they withdrew and returned prisoners, though it is possible

that they had been receiving monetary subsidies before this.
. . . The payment of subsidies was stopped in the afterglow
of Roman successes on the Danube front in the 240s,
which provoked a massive invasion by Goths and others
in 250.

And all through the later part of the third century AD, the Goths, at
the river-mouths of the western side of the Black Sea, continued to
be a nightmare to the Romans.

By the 230s at the latest, the federation began to assault the
provinces on the Lower Danube and Dacia, earning themselves subsidies thereby. The name 'Goths' was generally
applied to the aggressive grouping of warrior bands, but
almost certainly it included elements from numerous tribes.
The southward spread of the Goths is less likely to have
been a sudden migration *en masse* than a steady movement
into the rich lands of the south Russian steppe. When we
first hear of them they were threatening Moesia and Dacia
in the 230s and 240s. It was not long before the cities of the
Black Sea coasts and of Asia Minor experienced their
sweeping raids. . . .

In the middle of the third century, the Goths and their
associates were the most resourceful and threatening of the
enemies of Rome. They could strike deep into the rich
provinces of Asia Minor and range widely on naval expedi-
tions. They could attack the peaceful lands of Greece as well
as an exposed province like Dacia. But as yet they made no
concerted efforts to settle on Roman soil. The Black Sea
hinterland offered them enough land for settlement, and
raiding provided them with ample profit, for the time being.[7]

So the Romans, in the mid-third century, were very severely
menaced from the north and north-east.

3

THE PERSIANS

Unfortunately for Rome, the threat from the Germans was accompanied by an equally serious threat at the other end of the empire, from the Sas(s)anian Persians, who had supplanted their less formidable Arsacid predecessors in the 220s, and were ruled by one of the greatest men of the epoch, Sapor (Shapur) I (239 or 241–274), who towered above his Roman contemporaries, and led them a pretty dance.[1]

> Under the Sas(s)anids . . . Persia became once again a strong centralised monarchy . . . The stability of Sas(s)anian Persia was in marked contrast to the anarchy of third-century Rome. Indeed, between 226 and 379 only nine kings ruled Persia; during the same period there were some 35 Emperors at Rome.
> And the greatest of Sas(s)anid monarchs, Sapor [I], was a conqueror worthy to rank with Darius [I] or Cyrus [I the Great]. Roman and Persian sources are at variance about the wars fought by Sapor against Rome throughout his reign. . . . He invaded the provinces of Cappadocia and Syria on several occasions and . . . he captured Antioch at least twice. . . . Fortunately for Rome Sapor was no diplomat.[2]

Sapor was the name of kings of the Iranian (Sas(s)anid) dynasty, of which the most famous was Sapor I, son of Artaxerxes I (Ardashir) and co-regent with him 240–241. He continued, with spectacular success, his father's policy of aggression against Rome, taking full advantage of the internal crisis in the Roman empire. After Hatra (Al-Hadt) and the Roman outposts in Mesopotamia fell to the Sas(s)anians in the late 230s and early 240s, Gordian III started a counter-offensive, but was defeated in the battle of Misiche (near

Ctesiphon) (244), and died soon afterwards. The subsequent peace treaty between Sapor and Philip forced the Romans to pay a great deal of ransom. A further attack by Sapor led to the occupation of Armenia, the devastation of Syria, and the first conquest of Antioch (252–253). The third campaign of the Sas(s)anid 'King of Kings, King of Iran and non-Iran', as he called himself, saw the capture of Valerian (260) and Persian raids into Syria, Cilicia and Cappadocia. It was left to Septimius Odaenathus, dynast of Palmyra [Tadmor], to play a major role in forcing Sapor to withdraw from Roman territory (262–266). In addition to his military achievements (listed in his inscription at Naqsh-i-Rustam, the *Res Gestae Divi Saporis*, and depicted in his famous rock-reliefs), Sapor was honoured for his grandiose building operations (he used the labour of Roman captives), and for his relations with the religious leader Mani (founder of the Manicheans), who began his preaching in the Roman empire at the time of Sapor's investiture.

An additional word about the Sas(s)anians may be desirable.

> [They were] Kings of Iran AD 224–651. The dynasty derived its name from Sasan, the supposed grandfather of Artaxerxes I (Ardashir) in later Arab-Persian tradition. Though very often labelled heirs to the Achaemenids, they actually owed much more to the Parthians. Their empire at its greatest extent stretched from Syria to the Indus and from Iberia to the Persian Gulf. The Sas(s)anids constantly sought to alter the military *status quo* in the Mesopotamian, Armenian and Syrian areas; and the forts of the Euphrates *limes* were fortified against attacks from them by various Roman emperors. Diocletian and Galerius defeated [the Sas(s)anian] Narses in 297.[3]

The Sas(s)anid capital was at Ctesiphon (Taysafun).

Part 2

RECOVERY

4

STRONG EMPERORS

After the disastrous capture of Valerian (260), the Roman empire went from bad to worse. In the west, Postumus broke away, and since Odaenathus was virtually independent in the east, the imperial territory of Valerian's son Gallienus (253–268) was restricted to the central core of the empire. Yet Gallienus did much to save the Romans, because he reconstituted the army (see Chapter 5).[1]

However, the emperor Gallienus has been very variously estimated (see Figure 11). He has been considered to have 'ruled', if that is the right word, at the lowest time of the Roman empire. And, conversely, he has been considered its saviour, because, as stated above, he reorganised the Roman army. Both versions are true. The breach with Postumus did mean that the empire was disintegrating. But Gallienus did improve matters by his army reforms, which enabled the empire, in the long run, to survive. To take the first point first, the usurpation of Postumus (see Figure 12) was very serious for Rome.

> Postumus (Marcus Cassianius Latinius), Gallienus' military commander on the Rhine from AD 259, quarrelled with the young prince Saloninus [son of Gallienus] and his civilian advisers during the barbarian attacks following the capture of Valerian (260). He seized power and established himself a Roman emperor in Gaul, Britain and Spain. He defended his 'Gallic empire' against both Germanic invaders and Gallienus (268) . . .
>
> Postumus's strength and weakness was his determination not to march on Rome. This enabled him to defend the west, but strained the loyalty of his army and allowed no legitimate emperor to trust him entirely.[2]

Figure 11 Coin of Gallienus. (Photograph courtesy of Michael Grant).

Figure 12 Coin of Postumus. (Photograph courtesy of Michael Grant).

He abetted the revolt of Aureolus in 268, but had himself to meet the revolt of Laelianus in Moguntiacum (Mainz). He took the city, but was murdered by his own troops when he forbade its sack. His usurpation, as already suggested, saved the west.[3]

Yet Postumus 'weakened central authority', we are told. Indeed he did: this western state was quite separate from the empire of Rome. What with Odaenathus in the east – though not officially independent, in actuality he was – and Postumus in the west, the empire had broken up. It seemed doomed to destruction. Yet Gallienus, by his reconstitution of the empire's military strength, did, as has been said, a lot to save it from this fate. Here is his record and his career:

> Gallienus (Publius Licinius Egnatius), son of Valerian [was] appointed Augustus with him in AD 253. While his father lived, he commanded in the west and fought a series of successful campaigns on the Danube and Rhine.
>
> After the capture of Valerian by the Sas(s)anid Persians (260), he faced serious invasions and internal revolts. He dealt with the most threatening of these (the rebellion of Ingenuus, the Alamannic invasion of Italy, and the advance on Rome of Macrianus senior) with dispatch, making excellent use of the generals he had promoted through the ranks. He then adopted a policy of studied inaction, in effect accepting a tripartite division of the empire.
>
> In the east, Septimius Odaenathus of Palmyra first disposed of Gallienus' remaining opponents (Ballista, Quietus [the second son of Macrianus senior]), then, as *dux* and *corrector totius Orientis*, was allowed to supervise and defend the region in the emperor's name. In the west, Gallienus left the usurper Postumus in peace until the abortive campaign of 265, and did not trouble him thereafter. Gallienus thus gave himself the opportunity to consolidate his hold over his 'central' empire (Italy, North Africa, Egypt, the Danubian provinces and Greece) and pursue significant military, political, cultural and religious activities. In 268, however, he had to undertake a major campaign in the Balkans, where renewed Gothic invasions over the Black Sea and the Danube had, in 267, resulted in the sacking of Athens and other major Greek cities. He won an important victory on the Nestus [River Nesta], but was unable to exploit it because he had to return to northern Italy to deal with the mutiny of Aureolus. Though he quickly contained the insurrection, he was murdered by his staff officers as he besieged Aureolus in Mediolanum [Milan].
>
> The Latin literary tradition is uniformly hostile to

Gallienus, probably because he excluded senators from military commands. Modern scholarship tended to rehabilitate his reputation, stressing his recognition of the need for change (e.g. in professionalising the army, and making greater use of cavalry) and his prudent husbanding of scarce resources. Yet the disenchantment of his senior marshals – who owed their own careers to his patronage – indicates the need for caution, and recent studies have been more qualified in their assessment of him.[4]

Gallienus, when he was eventually murdered, was succeeded by Claudius II Gothicus (Marcus Aurelius) (268–270) (see Figure 13).

An equestrian cavalry general of modest Danubian stock, he owed his position to Gallienus' encouragement of men of talent, but was probably involved in the plot that overthrew his patron, and made him emperor (late summer 268).

He consolidated his rule by winning the support of both the ordinary troops and the senate – despite their quite different reactions to Gallienus' death and deification – by ridding himself of the usurper Aureolus, and by routing Germanic raiders in northern Italy. But Claudius' main concern was defence, and here he initially continued Gallienus' tactics, leaving the east to Palmyra and the Rhine

Figure 13 Coin of Claudius II Gothicus. (Photograph courtesy of Michael Grant).

to the Gallic empire, while himself concentrating on expelling the Goths from the Balkans. In this he was remarkably successful. His victory at Naissus [Niş] in 269 contributed significantly to removing the main Gothic threat for over a century: it is hardly surprising that Constantine I later claimed him as an ancestor. On the other hand, the next move [of Claudius II] would surely have been to reverse Gallienus' policy of *laissez-faire*, and attack either the Gallic empire (under Victorinus, less predictable) or Palmyra (under Zenobia, looking covetously at Egypt). However, before he could act he died of the plague in Sirmium [Sremska Mitrovica] (late summer 270).[5]

Claudius II Gothicus was succeeded by Aurelian (Lucius Domitius Aurelianus) (see Figure 14), *c.*AD 215–275, who was

a man of humble origin from the Danubian region, achieved high rank under Gallienus but helped organise the plot that destroyed him. Appointed by Claudius II to the chief command of the cavalry, he served with distinction against the Goths. Though Aurelian was the obvious successor to Claudius, he did not immediately declare himself on the latter's death, allowing the throne to pass to Quintillus. However, it was not long before he was hailed as emperor by his troops and disposed of his rival (*c.* September 270).

Barbarian invasions first claimed his attention. He defeated the Vandals in Pannonia and then repulsed a

Figure 14 Coin of Aurelian. (Photograph courtesy Michael Grant).

27

dangerous incursion into Italy by the Alamanni and Juthungi, pursuing the latter over the Danube. . . . With characteristic ruthlessness, he also disposed of early political opponents to his rule. He next dealt with Palmyra. . . . Marching back westward, Aurelian defeated the Carpi on the Danube, but was recalled by a further revolt in Palmyra (spring 273). He quickly crushed the uprising, and then proceeded to Egypt to suppress violent disturbances, possibly associated with the rebellion in Palmyra. Aurelian now turned west and ended the Gallic empire at Châlons [Catalaunian Plains], defeating Tetricus [I] (early 274). . . . Early in 275 Aurelian set out for Persia, but was murdered at Caenophrurium [Simekli], near Byzantium, in a household plot.

Aurelian's energy and military talents restored the unity of the empire after a decade of division, and he was more than just a successful general. Towards the end of his reign (274) he had the courage to abandon the old province of Dacia. . . . In many ways he pioneered the work of Diocletian and Constantine I. Yet he lacked the originality to bring the period of 'crisis' to its conclusion.[6]

Aurelian's relations with Zenobia, and his absorption of her realm, are interesting and important.

As long as Zenobia kept the east secure, Gallienus and Claudius II were prepared to accept her régime, including its bestowal upon Vaballathus [see Figure 15] of his father's Roman titles, and hence of the claim to be more than just king of Palmyra.

However, in 270 Zenobia exploited the political instability that followed the death of Claudius to expand beyond Syria by taking over Egypt and much of Asia Minor, and further to enhance Vaballathus' Roman titles, while continuing to recognise Aurelian as emperor. When Aurelian finally moved against her in 272, her forces failed to stop him at Antioch and Emesa [Homs], and – now calling her son *Augustus* and herself *Augusta* – she was besieged in Palmyra. She was captured while attempting to escape, shortly before the fall of the city.

She was spared. Many tales were told of her subsequent

Figure 15 Coin of Vabalathus (or Vaballathus). (Photograph courtesy of Michael Grant).

life; little is certain, though it is likely that she was paraded in Aurelian's triumph.[7]

Aurelian's general was killed while attempting to conquer Egypt, but he himself reoccupied Asia Minor with little resistance, defeated Zabdas, Zenobia's general, at Antioch and again at Emesa, and finally captured Palmyra and the queen herself and her sons. . . .

Zenobia is highly praised for her beauty, intelligence and virtue, but was evidently a ruthless woman. She sacrificed to her personal ambition the fortune of her native city, which Odaenathus had by his loyalty to the empire preserved.[8]

Aurelian started building walls round Rome.

To guard Rome against any repetition of such a threat as the invasion of the Juthungi, he [Aurelian] surrounded the capital with walls. The work, undertaken in consultation with the senate and with the assistance of guilds of city workmen, . . . only ended under Probus [276–282]. The new walls were not elaborate fortifications designed to stand a long siege, but a barely adequate defence against sudden barbarian attack.

The total length was twelve miles, the normal height twenty feet, the width twelve. There were eighteen gates, single or double, frequent sally-ports and towers for artillery. The walls in general followed the old Customs boundary. The plan of the work shows clearly that it was built by civilian labour: the hands of the soldiers were needed for other tasks.[9]

Aurelian, before leaving for the campaigns against Zenobia on the eastern frontiers, decided to protect Rome itself. . . . The wall so built was normally twenty-six feet high and twelve wide, provided with gates, posterns, towers for artillery, the whole having a circuit of some twelve miles, or eighteen point eight kilometres.

This would have prevented the capture and pillage of the city by a mobile force of barbarians; it was not meant to withstand siege by a civilised enemy.[10]

Despite a virtual mobilisation of the building industry the wall took about ten years to build. It was eleven and a half to thirteen feet (three and a half to four metres) thick at the base and in its original form twenty-five and a half feet (seven point eight metres) high, with a continuous open wall-walk, protected by a parapet and merlons. Square towers projected at intervals of one hundred Roman feet (ninety-seven English feet, or twenty-nine point six metres). In addition to numerous posterns there were eighteen principal gates, each with one or two stone arches flanked by two-storeyed semi-circular towers and surmounted by a windowed gallery to house the mechanism of the portcullis. Only the actual gateways were of stone. Elsewhere the material throughout is concrete faced with brick, almost all of it reused material. Evidently the organisation of the state-owned brick industry had broken down completely since Severan times.

No other monument so aptly symbolises the changed role of Rome within the empire. . . . Rome was only one of innumerable European cities which found themselves faced suddenly with the need to defend themselves in grim earnest against the menace from the north. The tide had turned, and was everywhere beginning to flow in reverse.[11]

In reality the [walls] were the first clear acknowledgment of a growing weakness . . . even the Urbs might be attacked by the barbarian. The walls . . . have been claimed – but on insufficient evidence – as showing the influence of eastern systems of fortification.[12]

The walls were begun in 270 or 271 after the incursion of a horde of German tribesmen into the Po valley had shown that even the capital of the Roman world could no longer afford to disregard its own defences. It was a vast undertaking.[13]

Aurelian was succeeded by Tacitus (Marcus Claudius) (see Figure 16), who only reigned for a short time.

An elderly senator, chosen to succeed Aurelian late in AD 275, he soon moved east and defeated the Goths who had invaded Pontus [N. Asia Minor], but in mid-276 he was killed by his own troops at Tyana [near Kemerhisar].

Tacitus made no attempt to restore senatorial authority in the face of the military: he may have been a veteran himself. The initial confusion of his reign, its brevity and its violent end, indicate continuing instability in the Roman empire, even after the reforms of Aurelian. [See Chapter 7.][14]

Figure 16 Coin of Tacitus. (Photograph courtesy of Michael Grant).

Figure 17 Coin of Probus. (Photograph courtesy of Michael Grant).

Tacitus certainly favoured the senate, but he did not give back to it the commands in the army. It was only the hopeful fancy of later historians that painted his reign as a late summer of constitutional government under the senate.

Tacitus was briefly succeeded by a man who was perhaps his half-brother, Florian (275), who was then succeeded by Probus (Marcus Aurelius) (see Figure 17).

Born at Sirmium [Sremska Mitrovica] in AD 232, [he] commanded the eastern army in 276. He challenged Florian after the death of Tacitus, and, as the better general, emerged as sole emperor (autumn).

He was an active warrior–emperor. In Gaul from 277 to 278, he expelled Alamannic and Frankish invaders, and restored the Rhine frontier. Between 278 and 280 he defeated the Burgundians and Vandals in Raetia and campaigned on the Middle Danube [see Chapter 2]. In 280 he moved to Antioch, where he directed the suppression of Isaurian banditry and nomadic incursions into Upper Egypt. His main intention was probably to deal with the Persian question, but he soon had to leave Syria to subdue mutinies on the Rhine and in Britain. Another rebellion, by Saturninus, in his rear, also failed. In 281 he celebrated a Triumph in Rome. In 282 he was at Sirmium when Carus claimed the purple in Raetia. Probus was killed by his own troops (autumn).

His problems with the army suggest growing military discontent. This is traditionally ascribed to Probus' disciplinarian tendencies and his use of soldiers as labourers on agricultural and civil engineering needs. Indeed, although in his military, civil and religious policies he projected himself as the authentic successor of Aurelian, his end is reminiscent of that of Gallienus. His main historical significance is his acceleration of the settlement of barbarians on Roman territory.[15]

The stern discipline of Probus and his employment of troops on the planting of vineyards were both unpopular. The danger of settling barbarians in the empire was revealed by the exploit of a band of Franks, who made their way home after extensive ravages in the Mediterranean. Probus sought the cooperation of the senate in government, but did not take the decisive step of putting senators back into military commands.[16]

Probus was succeeded by Carus (Marcus Aurelius) (see Figure 18).

Praetorian prefect from Narbo [Narbonne], [he] overthrew Probus after rebelling in Raetia, in AD 282. Leaving his elder son, Carinus, as Caesar in the west, Carus marched against

Figure 18 Coin of Carus (Marcus Aurelius). (Photograph courtesy of Michael Grant).

Persia with [his younger son] Numerianus. He captured Ctesiphon [Taysafun], but, advancing further, was killed, perhaps by treachery (summer 283).

He was the first emperor not to seek the senate's approval of his accession.[17]

On the way [to the east] he defeated the Quadi and Sarmatae on the Danube. Carus invaded Persia and captured Ctesiphon, but, venturing on a further advance, was killed, perhaps by treachery on the part of Aper, the praetorian prefect.[18]

Carus was briefly succeeded by his sons Carinus and Numerian; the latter was murdered, and the former was defeated by Diocletian (see Chapter 6).

5

THE ARMY
RECONSTITUTED

The reconstitution of the army, started by Gallienus, whose endeavours were mentioned in the last chapter, played a vitally important part in the recovery of the empire:

> By *c.*200 the old differentiation of recruitment between legionaries and auxiliaries had disappeared or become nominal. . . . Since there were numerous legions in the east . . . local recruiting was larger still. . . . Consequently the predominant element in the Roman army came from the warlike population of the Danubian provinces.
>
> The earlier idea of an indeterminate, variable, invisible frontier protection zone [came to be replaced] by the doctrine of fixed and fortified barriers. . . . [But] Gallienus, threatened not only by all manner of external invaders but by the dissident western empire of Postumus, took the important step of creating a field army of cavalry, which was intended to serve simultaneously as a reserve and a mobile striking force. Its principal base was Mediolanum [Milan], located at a convenient distance from the frontiers and Rome alike. This strategic centre, rapidly becoming even more important than the capital, was joined to Aquileia, Verona and Ticinum [Pavia] in a new system of north Italian defence necessitated by the loss of the upper Rhine–upper Danube area.
>
> But the new plans differed from the old static protection because they were conceived in terms not only of fortresses but of the newly created cavalry army. This élite force consisted of squadrons (we do not know how many) which were mostly five hundred men strong. They included heavy Persian-style cavalry, looking like knights of the Middle

Ages in their conical Iranian helmets, which the Germans later inherited; and an almost medieval concept of knighthood was to be seen in the hereditary gold ring granted to the sons of its centurions. Other elements in this army were Osrhoenian and Palmyrene mercenary archers on horseback, javelin-throwing Mauretanian riders, and a novel and valuable corps of mounted Dalmatians whose Illyrian origins guaranteed loyalty to Rome and leavened the exoticism of the other contingents.

This new arm of the service was celebrated by coins of Gallienus displaying the winged horse Pegasus, to whom a dedication is offered as the spirit of alertness (ALACRITATI). Other slogans speak of the courage of the cavalry (VIRTVS EQVITVM); and there are appeals to their loyalty (FIDEI EQVITVM) [see also below]. . . . Yet the commanders of this formidable cavalry army, necessarily men of ability, were under great temptation to revolt. . . .

Aurelian . . . employed his expert knowledge to operate light horse successfully against the massive mailed cavalry of Zenobia. Nevertheless, he also strengthened his own heavy cavalry on a large scale. . . . Diocletian proceeded to a military reorganisation of far-reaching variety and scope. Pursuing his predecessors' concern with mobile formations, he not only created a new barbarian mounted bodyguard (*scholae*), but made the field force into one of the two major parts into which the entire army was now divided. . . . Diocletian [also] reverted to earlier preoccupations with frontier defence. . . . Whereas Septimius' army [193–211] had totalled between 300,000 and 400,000 men, Diocletian's consisted of 500,000 or even more. . . . He was . . . particularly eager to make use of the warlike tastes and varying specialist skills of barbarian tribesmen. The soldiers mobilised from this almost inexhaustible source of supply included . . . Anatolians, who were to be the backbone of Byzantine armies; and many Germans.[1]

So even in the unprecedented and apparently desperate circumstances with which he was faced, Gallienus had found time to give a new shape to his army. The Romans had long since made use of mounted javelin-men and archers, and for over a century past they had also employed certain heavily armoured units of horse. But now the formidable heavy cavalry with which the Persians and Sarmatians were confronting them demonstrated that this branch of the army needed extension on a very large scale. And so Gallienus took the significant step of creating a major cavalry corps (264–8) [partly intended, too, to stave off usurpers]. This corps, a very expensive institution since a horse's feed cost as much as a soldier's rations, was intended to serve not only as a striking force but as a central military reserve, which had so long been lacking until [Septimius] Severus [193–211] made a start by his expansion of the military establishment in Italy at the end of the previous century. The principal base of the new army was Mediolanum [Milan]. Located at a convenient equidistance both from the frontiers and from Rome, this centre rapidly assumed even greater practical importance than the venerable capital.

The coins of Gallienus appeal to various virtues of the new élite force . . . and in particular [as we have seen] to its loyalty. . . . [O]ne of the large gold medallions, which it had become customary to hand out to high-ranking officers as personal rewards, was now bluntly inscribed 'Because you have remained loyal' (OB FIDEM RESERVATAM). In order to keep the officers of the new cavalry corps in this blessed condition, they were enrolled by Gallienus, together with a number of other officers, in a select staff group of household troops (*protectores domestici*), who encamped in the proximity of the emperor himself, and were attached to his own person. Nevertheless, it was precisely over this matter of loyalty that the new army reform proved most vulnerable.[2]

Gallienus's mobile army was 30,000 strong. Diocletian (284–305), as we have seen, also reformed the army.

As part of a large-scale reorganisation in many fields, he [Diocletian] and his fellow-Tetrarchs extensively overhauled the entire structure of the army.

Pursuing his predecessors' interest in mobile formations, he created a new barbarian mounted bodyguard, named *scholae palatinae* after a portico in the palace where they awaited imperial orders. These *scholae* were incorporated into one of the two major branches into which the entire army was now divided, the field force (*comitatenses*, 'soldiers of the retinue'). This mobile force, of which each of the four rulers controlled his own section, included infantry units, but it was in cavalry that its particular strength appeared. The second major division of Diocletian's armed forces was the frontier force (subsequently known as *limitanei* or *riparienses*), stationed along the strengthened fortifications of the borders.

The total strength of the Roman army was now half a million, perhaps about 20 per cent larger than the army of [Septimius] Severus a century earlier. It was recruited by systematic annual conscription among Roman citizens. But extensive use was also made of the warlike tastes and various specialist skills of barbarian tribesmen. These included numerous Germans, as well as men from the highlands of Asia Minor. . . . Diocletian also reorganised the navy, adding a number of small provincial fleets.[3]

The corps of *limitanei*, directing much improvised fortifications, consisted largely of Germans, with the addition of other barbarians of military qualities, and drafts of Roman conscripts, and mountain people from Asia Minor. This greatly increased army had to be paid for, and Diocletian introduced forcible measures to do so.

The measures taken by Diocletian were carried still further by Constantine.

Subject to criticism, despite his military talents, is Constantine's reorganisation of the army. From now on, it was divided between a frontier force and a striking force. There had been signs of this division before, but Constantine made it definitive. And there are reasons to suppose that it was a mistaken and disastrous decision, which helped to let the Germans in. Another thing that let them in was the increased admission of Germans into the army, both as top generals and as very numerous rank-and-file soldiers – again not a new development, but again they appear on an unprecedented scale. And, above all, Constantine enlarged and extended earlier policies that allowed German civilians to immigrate into the empire in thousands.[4]

Illyrian generals were also powerful during this period.

6

DIOCLETIAN

The rapid succession of emperors who began the recovery of the Roman Empire was discussed in Chapter 4. The process was completed – although by now the empire had become a very different place – by Diocletian (see Figure 19).

Diocletianus (Gaius Aurelius Valerius, 284–305) [was] originally named Diocles. Of obscure origins, [he was] born in Dalmatia, perhaps in the 240s AD. He rose to command the *domestici* (bodyguard) of the emperor Numerianus on the Persian campaign of 283–4. When Numerian was killed by his praetorian prefect Aper, the army proclaimed Diocles Augustus at Nicomedia [Izmit] (20th November 284). He killed Aper. He campaigned (285) against Numerian's brother Carinus, who was killed at Margus [Oraşjea Sredereva]. Maximian was made Augustus and spent the next years defending Gaul.

Diocletian spent most of his reign on the Danube or in the east. In 287 he installed Tiridates III as king of Armenia and reorganised the Syrian frontier. He campaigned on the Raetian frontier (288); he fought the Sarmatians (285 or 289) and the Saracens (290).

But the problems of the empire remained serious. On 1st March 293 he established the Tetrarchy [see below]. . . . In practice the empire was divided into two: Maximian and Constantius ruled the west, Diocletian and Galerius the east. Diocletian employed Galerius in Oriens [the east] until 299, thereafter on the Danube. Diocletian defeated the Sarmatians (294), and campaigned against the Carpi (296); many Bastarnae and Carpi were settled on Roman soil. . . . He sent Galerius to deal with the situation on the Syrian

Figure 19 Coin of Diocletian (Gaius Aurelius Valerius). (Photograph courtesy of Michael Grant).

frontier: the Persian king Narses had expelled Tiridates [III] from Armenia. Though defeated in his first campaign, Galerius won a total victory (298) and added significant territories to the empire. Campaigning by Constantius continued on the Rhine, but from 298 there was a general lull in rebellions and wars.

Tetrarchic authority was secure. Diocletian pursued systematically a long-established policy of dividing provinces into smaller units. . . . The army and the increase of administrative personnel were a heavy financial burden. Diocletian reformed the system of taxation. . . . Diocletian's genius was as an organiser – his measures did much to preserve the empire in the fourth century and lasted much longer in the east.[1]

Diocletian . . . gave the empire a new lease of life. Although the new empire of Diocletian was almost as strong as the empire had been in the days of Septimius Severus [193–211], it was vastly different. To maintain the control Diocletian sought and the times required, it was necessary to impose on the ancient Mediterranean civilisation an onerous bureaucracy in which the regulation of earlier days finally approached regimentation.[2]

This must not be forgotten: for those who lived in it, the revived empire, under a ruler who seemed more a godlike Pharaoh than a Roman magistrate, was intolerably worse than it had been, partly because of the much increased and stabilised taxation, which the relatively few *curiales* enforced rather than controlled.

> The reign of Diocletian is one of the last great milestones in the history of Rome. For there was hardly one speck of imperial civilisation that the reforming hand of Diocletian left untouched.
>
> And what he created or refurbished provided the political, military and economic institutions by which the empire survived in the west for another two centuries, and in the east, in the guise of the Byzantine empire, for another millennium.[3]

> In 293 Diocletian converted his dual regime, under himself and Maximian, into a Tetrarchy – a system envisaging the joint rule of two Augusti (himself and Maximian) and two Caesars. These Caesars, once again of Danubian origin, were . . . Constantius I [Chlorus] and Galerius, serving as junior colleagues to Maximian (in the west) and himself (in the east) respectively.
>
> Each of the Tetrarchs had his own separate capital city, adorned with splendid buildings. . . . This new arrangement . . . was planned both to satisfy military requirements and to ensure, when the time came, an orderly progress of joint accessions to the imperial office.[4]

> The arrangement was reinforced dynastically. Constantius, who already had a son, Constantine [later the Great] by Helena, was married to Maximian's daughter Theodora, and Galerius to Diocletian's daughter, Valeria. A more formal division of territorial responsibility was also instituted. . . . The death of Constantius in York [Eburacum] in 306 ended the Second Tetrarchy and precipitated a crisis.

It has already been mentioned that although the Tetrarchs had separate capitals, unity of the empire was strenuously emphasised.

Constantius [I Chlorus] established himself at Augusta Trevirorum (Trier).

> When Constantius chose it as his capital, the city was still suffering from the effects of a disastrous incursion of the Franks and Alamanni in 275–6. . . .
>
> Constantius now started to lay out, and Constantine [I the Great] completed, a palace complex occupying many *insulae* [blocks] in the north-east part of the town.

The capital of Galerius was at Thessalonica (Salonica).

> Thessalonica, strategically situated on the Via Egnatia, the main Roman land route from Italy to the Bosphorus and Asia, was already a town of importance. . . .
>
> To accommodate his palace Galerius added a whole new quarter on either side of it, along the eastern edge of the existing city. . . . Of the palace itself little is known beyond the fact of its position alongside the hippodrome.[5]

Surely looming very large in the minds of Constantine and his advisers lay the accumulated experience of the last fifty years, gained at Antioch, at Nicomedia (Izmit), at Thessalonica, at Sirmium (Sremska Mitrovica), at Milan, and at Augusta Trevirorum (Trier). In the late pagan architecture of these cities the old distinction between east and west, between capital and province, and between one province and another, had already gone far towards losing their meaning.[6] This was partly because of the Tetrarchical capitals. But there was also important building at Rome itself, of which the Baths of Diocletian survive, to a large extent, today (see also Chapter 6).

> Diocletian's great bath-building on the high ground north-east of the Viminal was begun in or soon after 298 and completed in 305–6. It followed closely the scheme established by the Baths of Caracalla. . . . If the latter building had marked the coming of age of the most ambitious of all imperial building types, the Baths of Diocletian certainly represent its full maturity.
>
> From the outside, the Baths relied for their effect almost exclusively on the marshalling of the masonry masses. The interior on the other hand was as rich and varied as the

exterior was simple . . . . Like the Pantheon, this is a building to be experienced, not described.[7]

Everything about the Baths of Diocletian is on a colossal scale: a labour force of 40,000 is said to have worked on them: 3,000 bathers could be accommodated at a time, and could find within their walls all the amusements of a major spa.

The reforms of Diocletian . . . brought a new period of comparative prosperity, and the last great works of pagan architecture in a Rome which now counted less in the world.

The Baths of Diocletian, the largest in ancient Rome, are, paradoxically, both more and less altered than those of Caracalla. Much of the original vaulting still covers the central hall [S.M. degli Angeli], resting upon eight ancient columns of red granite topped by rich Corinthian capitals.

In Rome the greatest achievement of the Principate [of Diocletian] was the erection, in the incredibly short space of two years, of the Thermae [baths], which were built by Maximian, and called by him after his colleague Diocletian in gratitude for his association in the empire.

They are situated on the south-eastern spur of the Quirinal Hill, at its junction with the Viminal, where . . . the usual systematisation and levelling of the ground took place, besides the necessary expropriation of the old house that had occupied the site. . . .

The Baths of Diocletian resemble in plan those of Caracalla, but exceed them in size. . . . Nothing can exceed the strength and harmonious beauty of the construction. . . . The baths built from the epoch of the Severi onwards . . . were to a great extent intended for the poorer classes of the population, who then as now lived in the suburbs.[8]

This was a great effort to show that, whatever the capitals might be elsewhere, Rome was still of prime importance; the point was rammed home under Constantine I the Great (306–337).

7

COINAGE AND FINANCE

The reconstitution of the army (Chapter 5) was enormously expensive, but the currency was so weak that the heavy taxation that was necessary had to be served by contributions in kind. The Roman currency reached its lowest level under Gallienus, in whose reign the empire was flooded by coins which although ostensibly multiple *denarii* (*'antoniniani'*), were in fact made of bronze, mitigated by the lightest of silver washes.[1] Gallienus's reform of the army was unaccompanied by the necessary reform of the coinage. If you look favourably upon that emperor, it is possible to conclude that he would have reformed the currency if he had lived; but he did not.

Aurelian instituted a reform of the coinage, which temporarily arrested the decline of the financial system;[2] but did not achieve much else. A more radical change was introduced by Diocletian.

> In order to pay [the] large military establishment . . . Diocletian had to raise enormous taxes from the civilian population, increasing payments in cash and kind to the very utmost that the Roman world permitted. . . . Foodstuffs and other objects vanished from the markets, and inflation, which had been afflicting the empire for so long and so disastrously, resumed its uncontrollable course.
>
> In an attempt to check this tendency, Diocletian had already in about 294 instituted a radical reform of the coinage. . . . [The taxpayers] in the foregoing decades had been gravely affected by the irregular suddenness and unpredictability of the demands made by the imperial exchange. To remedy this, the entire tax-collecting process was unprecedentedly placed on a regular basis. . . . On paper, a thoroughgoing totalitarian state was brought into

existence – although there was, in practice, no means of bringing this mass of rules and prohibitions into total effect.[3]

A multiplicity of mints, already foreshadowed, was now confirmed.

The unity of the empire was recovered. The effort was surely unequalled, but, as has already been said, the price paid for it by the people was appalling. By such means Diocletian had 'stabilised' conditions enough to attempt a reform of the monetary system. The changes were greater than any that had taken place since the time of Augustus.[4] The coinage system of Diocletian was the model for all that succeeded it. But in itself it only achieved a partial success. The introduction of reliable denominations of gold and silver was a permanent gain. But the silver-washed bronze, which was certainly tariffed too high for its intrinsic value and was apparently used as legal tender for large amounts, was less satisfactory. Prices again rose to absurd heights. . . . Force was impotent to effect permanent improvement here. . . .

Diocletian found the currency hopelessly debased. . . .

In 294 Diocletian and his partners carried out a reform of the coinage more radical than any that had ever been attempted before. *Aurei* continued at 60 to the pound. . . . The *argentei* introduced by Caracalla were officially adopted . . . a revival of the old 'Neronian' *denarius*. These were supported by large copper coins, now known as *folles*, which contained a small percentage of silver and weighed *c*.10 gr. . . . As a currency, nevertheless, it was not stable. . . . When silver was increasingly debased, and especially when the *antoninianus* became almost pure copper in the middle of the third century, 'silver' – still in a fixed relationship with gold – to all intents and purposes became part of a dying token *aes* system.[5]

It was not until Constantine the Great (306–357) that the monetary collapse was arrested. I have devoted a book to his reign, but I should like to offer one quotation from it here:

[Constantine reconstructed] the administrative machine, in regard to which, despite his extraordinary abilities in this field, he can be blamed for over-taxation, extravagance, failure to prevent corruption, and coinage which favoured the rich. . . .

It must be concluded that Constantine's arrangements for taxation, although partly inherited and no doubt urgently required by the costly policies on which he had embarked, contributed largely to the future of trade and agriculture, and caused widespread hostility to the State. It was a crushing tax system, which ultimately defeated its own purpose, because it destroyed the very people who had to pay the taxes.[6]

As a numismatist, I must be excused if I devote a special section to the designs on the coinage of the period, in addition to what has

Figure 20 Coin of Maximian (Marcus Aurelius Valerius). (Photograph courtesy of Michael Grant).

Figure 21 Coin of Carausius. (Photograph courtesy of Michael Grant).

already been said. In general, of course, the rulers offer their own version of events, their own propaganda, on the coins (see Figures 20, 21 and 22). This is how C.H.V. Sutherland put it:

> For some decades after Severus Alexander, the coin-types of the 'legitimist' emperors lapsed into something like a routine dullness. Each in turn claimed the protection of heavenly *providentia*, looked to Jupiter and the other great gods as champions, restored *libertas*, distributed *liberalitates*, relied on the *fides* of the soldiers, and boasted of the *pax* won by *victoria*, leading to Triumph, general *laetitia, aequitas* (especially in the economy), and *securitas*; and there were of course the now traditional types for heirs and imperial ladies.

47

Figure 22 Coin of Constantius I. (Photograph courtesy of Michael Grant).

It was as if emperors who were insecure, and too often ephemeral, felt that those public announcements were best that adhered most closely to the great dynastic coinages of earlier times. The chief interest in their coinages was to be found partly in the portraiture, partly in the technical and economic history of production. Portraiture, indeed, continued at a generally very high level.

Usurpers . . . further weakened the strength of Rome. Already under Philip [244–9] there had been shadowy figures – Pacatian, Jotapian, Silbannacus, Sponsianus – who left a ripple on the face of history and of coinage. About 253–4 Uranius Antoninus set himself up briefly in the east at Emesa [Homs], coining in gold alone with types which, when they did not echo those of Rome, again celebrated the Emesan cult of the god Elagabalus. . . .

The Gallic provinces had normally in the past possessed a robust sense of individualism; and Postumus [266–270] expressed this clearly. He was fighting, as Mars, for a *Romanitas* threatened by weakness in the central government at Rome. . . . The propagandist impact of his abundant coinage, with its unequivocal types, must have been great, and all the greater for the skill with which it was produced.[7]

8

STATE RELIGION

The Roman imperial public was becoming more and more mono-theistic at this time.[1] Aurelian decided to revive the cult of the Sun, and to make it the hub of the whole of Roman religion. It was already honoured and revered by a number of disparate temples. Septimius Severus and his successors (as well as usurpers) had honoured it; Maximinis I Thrax had put up a monument to the god; and he had been glorified as 'Invictus' by Victorinus (268–276) and Probus (276–282).

> Like Elagabalus, Aurelian was importing into Roman cult the vigorous beliefs of partially Hellenised Syria, which were now so pervasively active in contemporary speculation. But his tactics were more statesmanlike than the earlier emperor. In this determined effort to revivify and concentrate paganism, Aurelian was not overturning the Roman cults; he was adding to them, and thereby changing their emphasis and balance of power, so that Sol now stood at the head of the pantheon.
> This was not only an integration, it was a creative, novel deed of religious statecraft. Aurelian's decision . . . sought to weave the main religious strands of east and west into a united, cosmopolitan, universal faith. . . . Since Aurelian reconquered Gaul as well as the east, his cult of Sun-Apollo may also have echoed the Gallic worship of gods of light and healing identified with Apollo.[2]

> Aurelian had shown great concern at the looting of Palmyra's [Tadmor's] Temple of the Sun, and had com-manded its restoration. In size and perhaps in plan this Temple on the Quirinal, whatever its date and origin,

showed the influence of the vast structures of Egypt and of Syrian Baalbek [Heliopolis]. Its columns are estimated to be fifty–eighty feet high, with capitals more than eight feet.[3]

It is said that Aurelian . . . roundly told his troops that it was not they, but the god, who assigned the imperial power. Herein may be seen one of the springs of that religious policy which Aurelian followed throughout his reign and crowned in 274 by the erection in Rome of a magnificent temple to the Sun-god and the establishment of a new college of senators as *pontifices dei Solis. Sol dominus imperii Romani* was to be the centre of revived and unified paganism and the guarantor of loyalty to the emperor, whose companion and preserver he was. . . . It was clearly the intention of Aurelian to make the most of the breadth and inclusiveness of his worship, in which Greek and Roman worshippers of Apollo might unite with eastern devotees of Mithras or Elagabalus, while, on the other hand, the form of the cult was Roman.[4]

Aurelian's . . . Temple of the Sun (Sol) was . . . symptomatic of its age. It reflects the . . . broadly monotheistic trend of religious thinking, eastern in origin, as was manifest also in Christianity. Even the dedication recalls such nearly contemporary monuments as the Christ-Helios mosaic of the Vatican cemetery and the Sol Invictus coinage of Constantine himself [306–337]. The occasion for the temple's foundation and the funds for its building were furnished by Aurelian's reconquest in 273 of Zenobia's short-lived oriental empire of Palmyra.

Of the classical buildings nothing is now visible. They lay just east of the modern Corso, beneath and near the Church of S. Silvestro, and our knowledge of them is derived almost entirely from a plan and drawing made by [Andrea] Palladio in the sixteenth century, when quite a lot must still have been standing. Palladio's plan shows a circular temple in the centre of a large rectangular enclosure.[5]

Aurelian's immediate predecessors, as well as earlier leaders, had done the ground-work with regard to the worship of Sol (the Sun).

Gallienus proposed to dominate the city, from the highest point of the Esquiline Hill, with a chariot group including a colossal statue of himself as the Sun. His successor Claudius II Gothicus (268–70) was devoted to the same deity, and then the logical, conclusive move was taken soon afterwards by the next emperor Aurelian. For he established, as the central and focal point of Roman religion, a massive and strongly subsidised cult of Sol Invictus (274), endowing him with a resplendent Roman temple, and instituting on the model of the ancient priestly colleges, and as their equal in rank, a new college of Priest of the Sun. . . .

In such developments several threads are apparent. First, official religion had long been moving in this direction. Secondly, Aurelian came from the Illyrian land of Pannonia, where Sun-worship is attested in the astral symbolism of many tomb reliefs; and his own mother was said to have been its priestess in their village. And then again his own name fortuitously, but felicitously, suggested a link with the family of the Aurelii which had traditionally been in charge of the ancient Sun-worship of Rome. Furthermore, Aurelius was deeply influenced by the Syrian veneration of the Sun. . . .

Aurelian now restored [the temple of Malachbel (Baal) [the Sun-god] at Palmyra, and interpreting its deity as a form of Sol Invictus, adorned his own Roman temple of the Sun with statues not only of Helios-Sol but also of Belos or Baal. . . . Sol now stood at the head of the Pantheon. . . .

The strongest part of Aurelian's army came, like himself, from Sun-worshipping Pannonia. . . . The cult was now officially prescribed for the army, and its symbols were added to military insignia.

In pursuance of a concept that had been developing for over a century, the Sun was the emperor's special comrade and companion. . . . Constantine [I Chlorus] was a mono-theist who revered the Sun, like his forebears before him in their Sun-worshipping Balkan homeland. Then in c.309 Constantius' son Constantine the Great began his vast, homogeneous series of coinages inscribed SOLI INVICTO COMITI. . . . These uniform, multitudinous issues . . . represented a huge scale operation unmistakably intended to implant an idea in the minds of the populations of the empire.[6]

Yet this did not work; Christianity, not Sun-worship, was the religion of the future.

> Why then did Sun-worship fail to remain the religion of the empire? Its most attractive features were simplicity and obviousness and ready justification: the Sun was there for all to see, and everyone could appreciate its indispensable, beneficial, creative activities. Moreover, although its abstract and learned side proved convenient to rulers as a theology on which to base their own domination, the cult was not limited to intellectuals and the governing classes; for there were no more passionate Sun-worshippers than the ordinary unintellectual soldiers of the Roman army.
>
> And yet the creed was deficient in profundity, emotional intimacy and heartening humanity. It did not grapple with the problem of evil. . . . It was weak in the appeals which endeared the mystery religions to millions. It also lacked two allurements which were the strength of Christianity: the explicit praises of immortality which cheered poor people in desperate times, and the excitement of a Messiah who was believed to have been an actual historical figure. . . .
>
> Meanwhile . . . [an] attitude to Sun-worship, more deeply rooted in religious feeling, enjoyed . . . success in providing the personal, emotional, dramatic satisfaction which the Sun cult, for all its imposing simplicity, lacked. This was Mithraism, which also linked solar theology with the other outstanding pagan movement of the time, the dualism of good and evil power.[7]

Constantine's attitude to Sun worship was significant, but ambiguous. Underneath St Peter's, as we have seen, there is a mosaic on which Jesus is represented as the Sun-god.

> Constantine felt a strong need for a divine companion and sponsor, and for a time the Sun, whose worship had been ancestral in his family, was his choice. . . . It was athwart the Sun that he claimed to have seen the Cross, and on the sculptures of the Arch of Constantine at Rome the old gods have gone but the Sun still remains: the emperor is represented between the rising Sun and the moon, and the victory-giving figure is the Sun-god, whose statuettes are carried by the army's standard-bearers. An inscription

describes Constantine himself as the Sun who sees all. It was not until 318–319, when the Christianisation of the empire had gathered force, that the Sun disappeared from the coinage. . . .

Christians in east and west, in their public and private prayers, turned to Oriens, the rising Sun, in order to glorify its resurrection from the prison of the dark, which they identified with the Resurrection of Christ. . . . Some people confused the two deities. . . . That is partly why devotees of the Sun . . . were among the fiercest enemies of the Christians. . . . St Leo the Great (d.461) complained that Christians still worshipped the Sun.[8]

[Constantine] was a Christian of a very peculiar type that would hardly be recognised as Christian today. For the God he believed in was a God of power, who had given him victory, and he would have had little sympathy with the idea that Christianity meant love, or charity, or humility, of which his 'middle-brow' view of religion would not have the slightest comprehension.

Furthermore, he was utterly confident that he himself was the man of God, God's servant and representative who was constantly in touch with Him and was told by Him what to do. . . . This made Constantine a difficult man for other mere human beings to deal with; being on a direct line with God, he must always be right. . . . [But] it became clear very soon that Christianity was hopelessly divided within itself.[9]

Nevertheless, Christianity, however much divided, had defeated Sun worship as the cult of the future.

Part 3

AWAY FROM POLITICS

9

PHILOSOPHY AND
PERSONAL RELIGION

Political (and military) life at this period was so intolerable (and, let us face it, boring) that many turned to quite other matters in order to take their minds off what was happening at the top. This was particularly true of the *intelligentsia*, or upper class. There were several main channels for this sort of escape: the religions, philosophy, and the novel or romance. Religion had been partly taken over by the State (cf. last chapter). But it could not take over philosophy, which was still particularly active at Athens, while Berytus (Beirut) and Apamea (Qalaat al Mudik) were also active, and Antioch was not mediocre. But one of the most widely read writers of the period seems to have come from Egypt. This was the Neoplatonist philosopher Plotinus (AD 205–269/70) (see Figure 23). He has been written about in the following terms:

> The main facts of his life are known from Porphyry's memoir (prefixed to editions of the *Enneads*). His birthplace, on which Porphyry is silent, is said by Eunapius and the *Suda* to have been Lyco or Lycopolis in Egypt. But his name is Roman, while his native language is almost certainly Greek.
>
> He turned to philosophy in his twenty-eighth year, and worked for the next eleven years under Ammonius Saccas at Alexandria. In 242–3 he joined Gordian III's unsuccessful expedition against Persia, hoping for an opportunity to learn something of eastern thought. The attempt was abortive, and at the age of forty he settled in Rome as a teacher of philosophy, and remained there until his last illness, when he retired to Campania to die.
>
> At Rome he became the centre of an influential circle of intellectuals, which included men of the world and men of

Figure 23 Head of Plotinus. (Museo Ostiense Sala XI. Archivio
Fotografico della Soprintendenza Archeologica di Ostia).

letters, besides professional philosophers like . . . Porphyry. He interested himself also in social problems, and tried to enlist the support of the emperor Gallienus for a scheme to found a Platonic community on the site of a ruined Pythagorean settlement in Campania. Plotinus wrote nothing until he was fifty.[1]

Plotinus saw living reality as a complex, ordered, hierarchical structure which continuously proceeds from its transcendent First Principle, the One or Good, descending . . . from this supreme power through the Divine Mind and then the Soul to the last and lowest reality, the Body. . . . Men's life, like the universe, is an upward yearning urge. . . .

He is the pioneer of psychedelic experience for the west, but he achieved his end by purely cerebral, intellectual discipline – not by schizophrenia and not by drugs, and not by religion. . . . The moral and social implications of his doctrine have sometimes inspired repugnance. . . . Plotinus' world was no ivory tower but reality at its highest level, raised to its most exalted plane by the intensest concentration on what seemed to him the most real. . . . Union with the One is to tackle life with a daring and dedicated brand of realism. . . .

Within this living, organic cosmos . . . there are two great movements – an outgoing downward surge from the One, and an upward Return. . . . This procession moves on its majestic, everlasting path by self-contemplation. . . . Man can realise his one self by voluntary self-identification with the source. . . .

The One, as he conceived it, is beyond thought or definition of language: it inhabits summits where reason, bewildered as in a storm, forsakes even thought. . . . By the analogy of the self-contemplation of the One, Mind is likewise both thought and the object of thought. . . . Below Mind is the universal Soul. . . . Each individual is himself in his own right. . . . 'What am I?'

For there was a crisis of identity in the vast tumultuous Roman empire as in the teeming communities of our own western world. . . .

[The] world of the senses is essential to the nature of things, regrettable and vexatious no doubt, yet requiring to be accepted. . . . 'Turn from the things without to look within. The sum of things is within us'. . . . We advance towards the God by 'the sternest and uttermost combat'.[2]

For those of a more directly religious turn of mind there was Mani and Manichaeanism.

> In *c*.240 . . . the young Mani started to preach at the Persian (Sassanian) capital Ctesiphon (Kut), and Seleucia which lay opposite it across the Tigris. A contemporary of the other spiritual personality of the century, Plotinus, Mani taught for thirty years. By the time of his death, the Persian empire was filled with Manichaean doctrines, and within the following centuries they had permeated huge regions of the Roman empire. . . .
>
> His teaching conveys the basic dualism in which Persian and Greco-Roman strands converge. . . . His movement had its heart in Mesopotamia and Syria and western Asia. . . . [The Manichaeans] were an unstable and even a socially revolutionary element on the sensitive Persian frontier. . . . Nevertheless during the century after Mani's death his doctrines became a world religion; nearly *the* world religion.[3]

Manichaeanism – in the sense that there is believed to be a continual fight between God and the Devil – is still today the faith of millions of ordinary people, if they only knew it. This forceful doctrine survived from the third . . . century, demanding from its adherents an absolute belief in the distinction between Good and Evil. Both were eternally co-existent. . . . This dualism, known as Gnostic (from *gnosis*, knowledge), was reputed to go back to Simon Magus. . . . Most of [the] sects eventually became merged in Manichaeanism. . . . Mani established an elaborate, well-organised Church and . . . planned to found a spiritual community that would conquer the entire world. . . .

> Diocletian . . . introduced savage sanctions against the Manichaeans . . . apparently regarding them as potential instruments of Rome's Persian foes.[4]

Manichaeanism failed to become the world religion, which Christianity became. We can understand why.

[The Manichaean] martyrs lacked the dramatic appeal of the Christians. . . . They were too anti-social to create a National Church. . . . Nor did [Manichaeanism] fully satisfy the spiritual emotions of the time. . . . Augustine felt it nobler and more rewarding to make the effort of faith demanded by Christianity. . . . It . . . had been launched by a series of alleged historical happenings which the vague myths of the Manichaeans could not rival. . . . [And] in spite of Mani's global aspirations, he preached a perfection to which only an elect of initiates could aspire. Christianity, too, went through such phases of esotericism . . . but it outgrew them and intensified its appeal.[5]

So Christianity defeated and outlived both Manichaeanism and Sun-worship.

10

HELIODORUS AND THE
AETHIOPICA

It seems likely, however, that many Romans and Greco-Romans, instead of adopting Manichaeanism or Christianity, preferred to read novels or romances. Whether this applied chiefly to women, as has been asserted, we do not know, but feel inclined to doubt: surely men read novels too, as they do today. And indeed, political and military goings-on were so depressing and wearisome that many people belonging to what might be described as the intelligentsia turned not only to religion but to the novel. In particular, in the later third century, they read Heliodorus, who was the last of the great novelists: they read his *Aethiopica*.

These novel readers formed an important and interesting part of the community.

> We could be led into thinking that we must picture the novel's reader as someone of little learning and accordingly low social standing. . . . However, our scant knowledge of the social structure of ancient readerships poses a serious hindrance to finding the definitive answer on this point. Only this much can be said with any degree of certainty: the number of people who were able and could afford to read a book purely for entertainment was still quite small, and comprised for the most part members of the upper and middle class. Within this group, novels quite probably even enjoyed a certain popularity. . . .
>
> [But] the ancient novels could offer something for all tastes. . . . Most of the surviving texts offer a strikingly large variety of opportunities for women readers to identify with the characters in the story. . . . [We can point to] the frequent portrayal of the heroines as more active, more

intelligent and more likeable than their often more colour-
less lovers.[1]

Meanwhile the Greek middle-brow novel had come very much
into its own, and women, naturally, fill its pages. For the novel
focused on a love relationship in which due attention is paid to the
female partner, a young man and his fiancée or wife, whose
reciprocal faithfulness, rectitude and courage are tested by one
tribulation after another; finally, all these hazards are overcome
and they live happily ever after.

A recent and standard study of later Greek literature places
the novel in the category of *le nouveau*, part of the creative
effort of the Hellenistic age. As such it can be felt as
something not quite conceivable in the political world
before Alexander the Great . . . a hybrid, some sort of
subliterary mutant pieced together from the spare parts of
respectable literature in response to popular taste, with no
inner life-force of its own. . . .
    At last we are in a position to see the ancient novels in a
different perspective. The extended romantic tales that
underlie them go back at least to Sumerian times. . . . It
is as the artful retelling of ancient tales, rather than the
random invention of ephemera, that ancient prose fiction
may best be understood and enjoyed. . . . The novels can
no longer be dismissed . . . as the products of literary
triflers and nonentities in an age of decadence.[2]

A leisurely elaboration . . . is especially manifested in the
construction of dramatic set-pieces. Time and trouble are
applied to development of plot and delineation of character
alike. The work [*Aethiopica*] is held by many to be the best of
the extant novels. Motivation is well handled, the principal
characters nicely drawn – even if they may not achieve the
realism of Achilles [Tatius, 2nd century], and the sub-plots
and digressions in which the . . . author takes pleasure are
carefully integrated in the story. But it is in the story itself,
and the manner in which Heliodorus unfolds its complex-
ities, that his superiority most clearly lies. . . .
    Heliodorus' Odyssean plunge *in medias res* not only gives
pace and tension to the story but allows the structure to be
presented to the readers from different angles. . . . It is as a

product of the literary skills of the Sophistic age operating in their most developed form upon the range of models open to writers of prose fiction that the *Aethiopica* is best seen.[3]

> The *Aethiopica* [is] the longest and best of the extant Greek novels. . . . What makes Heliodorus excel over other Greek romancers is his narrative technique: he superbly masters the development of the plot which in spite of its amplitude and complexity never becomes confused. The reader['s] . . . attention is immediately and permanently captivated. Through flash-backs, appropriate concatenation of accessory episodes and surprises intervening at the right moment, the tension is never relaxed. The work is free from licentiousness and pervaded with sincere faith in Heliodorus' . . . religion. The characterisation, however, is weak, the personages being guided throughout by the god Helios (the Sun), who is identified with Apollo. The diction is pure Attic, but literary pretensions are evident in the use of daring metaphors and *recherché* expressions. Apt quotations and allusions show a wide literary knowledge.[4]

The position of women in the novel has already been mentioned. And it is particularly strongly stressed by Heliodorus.

> The innovation in the *Aethiopica* is the energetic and resourceful companionship provided by Charicleia to her lover. In many crises it is she who takes the lead and is a more inventive thinker than the brave, but easily discouraged, Theagenes. . . . Here is a woman, almost for the first time in literature, assuming her proper status as the friend and companion of men. . . . Another profound concern of Heliodorus was to show the divine guidance behind this love. . . . In particular, he reveals a lofty conception of the Sun-god, felt to be universal and identified with Apollo. . . . Despite every incidental set-back, the gods are helping and guarding their special charge. . . . We must put aside the modern idea that religion and entertainment are incompatible.[5]

The central figure [of the *Aethiopica*] is Charicleia, born white and therefore exposed by her mother the Ethiopian

[Aethiopian] queen. Conveyed by a travelling Greek, Charicles, from Ethiopia to Delphi and there given a good Greek education, she became priestess of Artemis [Diana], at whose festival she and a Thessalian aristocrat, Theagenes, fall in love. Aided by a priest from Memphis, Calasiris, searching for Charicleia at her mother's request, they elope, and after many novelistic adventures – pirates, brigands, lustful suitors, false deaths – they at last reach Ethiopian Meroe, where they escape being sacrificed, and Charicleia, recognised by her parents, marries Theagenes.

Heliodorus masterfully launches his reader into mid-story, with a bizarre scene of blood, bodies and booty on an Egyptian beach viewed through the eyes of mystified brigands. . . . Thereafter the linear narrative exploits surprise more than suspense, save that we always wonder if the couple will 'really' be reunited.

Recurrent metaphors from the tragic stage, and assessments, by characters and the author, of the gods' and Fate's role in the universe, invite us to read the work as elevated and deeply serious. . . . Yet in some scenes Grand Guignol trespasses on the comic. . . . The novel becomes a *tour de force* in which one literary trick succeeds another. . . . Heliodorus can be seen as variously parodying the genre . . . and the complexity, irony and suspense created by Heliodorus' opening *in mediis rebus*, and gradual unfolding of the couple's story through Calasiris' long and sometimes misleading narrative, mark him as a master of plot construction.[6]

[This is] the longest and best constructed of the Greek novels extant. [One passage] . . . seems to point to some family connexion with the Helios cult established in Emesa [Homs]. . . . [The] work is penetrated with sincere religious piety. . . . Heliodorus' characterisation is weak . . . he is lacking in sense of humour. . . . [But his] literary knowledge was unusually wide. . . . [He shows a] skilled and unsurpassed technique of narration. . . . The tension is never relaxed.[7]

EPILOGUE

As this book has shown, in the course of the third century AD the Roman empire nearly collapsed. There was everything against its survival. Emperors came and went thick and fast – usually they were murdered not very long after their accession – there was a host of usurpers at Rome and elsewhere, and there were extremely and unprecedentedly severe threats on the German and Persian frontiers. It must have been terrible to have lived in the Roman empire at that time. This great organisation, which had controlled every territory from the Atlantic to the Euphrates, seemed as if it had broken to pieces. And its collapse appeared to be irretrievable.

Nevertheless, the empire did not collapse, but survived. The western empire survived for another two hundred years, and more, and the eastern empire survived for twelve hundred years, with a brief intermission. This is an extraordinary story, which has partly escaped us. It has escaped us because the ancient accounts of what happened are incomplete, inadequate and biased, so that it has been very difficult to build up a modern account. In actual fact, the survival of the empire, in the face of intolerable odds, is something of a miracle, and one of the most remarkable phenomena in human history. Here was a ruined unit, and out of the ruins came another, different but equally formidable, empire. It is the task of the present book to outline this collapse and recovery. As already stated, there is not much that is reliable among the sources, but use can be made of what there is, and the result is startling. It will warn us not to trust too much in historical processes and apparent historical inevitability.

Dare one, also, link up this theme with modern affairs, as possibly relevant to some of our own predicaments? Certainly the Roman empire had very different boundaries from our own western world – which does not terminate at the Rhine, but much further east and north – and it is more than doubtful whether we can ever extend the western world as far to the south-east as the Romans did. Nevertheless, the Roman imperial phenomenon does ring a bell, because it does contain points of relevance to what is happening today, or rather to what will be happening before long. For what is likely to be happening, although not all of us will be alive to see it, is a confrontation between the western world and those outside it. It is not for me, now, to go into further details about this confrontation, but I do maintain that it is likely to occur. It also attacked the Roman empire, which was nearly destroyed: but not quite. It was saved because of its superior organisation. This meant that, in the end, it was able to overcome the enemies who had seemed so extremely likely to demolish it. The price was terrible; and so will the price be today. But the point at issue is survival – the Roman empire survived, and so, in all probability, will the West today.

For the ancient world had temporarily collapsed, and partially recovered by military means – at the cost of great hardship for individuals. What we owe that ancient world is enormous, and we often neglect it. The ensuing Roman empire that nearly collapsed has been the subject of many criticisms and attacks today. There is much talk of imperialist domination and exploitation. There are too many 'Great Men', and the 'Grandeur that was Rome' has been accused of being both jingoistic and racist (as well as sexist). On the other hand, the Romans did provide the peoples of many nations with baths, bridges, straight roads, and much else. And they were undoubtedly among our own predecessors. But their empire, as revived by Diocletian, displayed a good deal of evil that had not been there, to such a massive extent, previously: militarism, over-taxation, excessive bureaucracy, dictatorial autocracy. These are points which we may well wish to consider, before we establish the new Europe. We must try to avoid the mistakes the late Romans made, and found necessary to keep their 'civilisation' going.

APPENDIX

The Greek and Roman civilisations
that were now collapsing

The purpose of this Appendix is to outline, briefly, the story and
quality of the Greco-Roman civilisation which so nearly disappeared in the third century but was miraculously – and at such
great cost to the individual, as we have said – revived, and which,
despite many subsequent attempts at its rehabilitation, is in grave
danger of vanishing from view today, although, increasingly during
the century to come, it is likely to be the subject of profound and
relevant study again. Without this delineation the full significance
of the near collapse can scarcely be appreciated.

Even if, in this book, an attempt has been made to rehabilitate a
late period in the ancient world, which has tended to be forgotten
– owing to military preoccupations and a lack of ancient sources
(except by a devoted band of numismatists) – the wider point
remains: is there any point, nowadays, in studying the ancient world
at all? Let me say, yes.

However, the third century emperors, owing to the military
needs that have been mentioned, were not very interested in the
past of their Greco-Roman world. The only notable exceptions are
the rulers Gallienus (253–268), who admired the Hellenistic
achievements and was asked to help its contemporary representative Plotinus, and Tacitus (275–276), who claimed a relationship
with the historian of the same name. Otherwise, the past tended to
be forgotten from on high. Of course, there were inheritances: for
example, clothing tended to follow, with differences, an antique
model, and the Colosseum and the Forum of Trajan still stood in
Rome. Yet the past was past, and done with. Let us just recall,
however, what this past was, and what it signified; for it is still
relevant not only to the third century but to ourselves, as we have
seen.

HISTORY

In other words, this is probably the point at which something should be said about the great Greco-Roman tradition of which this book records the apparent collapse, even if it was followed by a partial recovery in a somewhat new form. The Greeks and Romans had really created something, which stood out as valuable in a world which was otherwise as un-Greco-Roman as most of the world is today. This creation had undergone a long history of development, and it is surely of value here to outline the main features of the past, since it was these that were now being lost, or changed beyond most recognition – although many of these features have, to some extent, been revived so that they still form a bastion against the outside world nowadays.

After the periods of the Minoans (centred upon Cnossus in Crete) and the Mycenaeans (who take their name from Mycenae in the Argolid [Peloponnese]), the Bronze Age Civilisation had come to an end, in the final centuries of the second millennium BC, and Greek history proper may be said to have begun. In particular, the Dorians broke into the Peloponnese, where unified Sparta was probably the first authentic city–state, and Ionians, after whom the western coastlands of Asia Minor are named, were said to have been linked with the foundation of Athens. The whole subsequent course of Greek history was dominated by the strife between the land empire of Sparta and the sea empire of Athens. In Homer, the alleged author of the *Iliad* and the *Odyssey*, Ionian elements predominate. The date of the two wonderful poems remains uncertain, but they were apparently composed before 700 BC, although they look backwards in time.

The Ionians of Asia Minor, led by Miletus (Balat), sailed into the Black Sea and established their first colonies on its shores in the first half of the eighth century BC. The Ionians of Chalcis and Eretria in Euboea opened up the west, in the middle of that century, by establishing colonies on the island of Pithecusae (Ischia) in the Cumaean Gulf (Bay of Naples) and at Cumae itself on the mainland opposite. They were also the earliest Greek colonisers of Sicily. The Dorians then founded important and durable colonies. Thus Corinth created Syracuse and Corcyra (Corfu), Megara founded Byzantium, and Sparta established Taras (Tarentum). Greek colonisation continued until *c*.550 BC, and was only limited by the rival sea-powers of Egypt, Phoenicia and the Etruscan states.

Greek prosperity caused the claims of birth to be upset by the claims of wealth, and the result was the establishment of dictatorships (tyrannies). The lead was taken by Corinth (c.657–c.582 BC), followed by Sicyon and (briefly) by Megara. The fall of the tyrants inaugurated a period of convulsion and bitterness. In some city–states, however, the troubles that were caused by the growth of prosperity were solved by 'law-givers' or arbitrators. The most famous of these was Solon of Athens, who gave each section of the State those powers which he regarded it as able to wield, and ascribed to every Athenian citizen freedom of person, equality before the law, influence in election and government, and a certain amount of economic strength; although he left real power in the hands of the well-born members of the Council of Areopagus and, like other ancients, did not touch slavery on which the State was ultimately based.

After Solon had left the scene there was a prolonged time of party strife at Athens which came to an end when Pisistratus finally seized power in c.546 BC. He and his sons Hippias and Hipparchus made Athens one of the principal commercial centres of the Greek world, notable for its black-figure and then red-figure 'vases'. The Spartans employed force to expel Hippias in 510 but were themselves expelled from Athens by a returned exile, Cleisthenes, who became 'law-giver' and safeguarded the political and electoral rights of every citizen, while leaving the constitution in the hands of those who had the experience to look after it.[1]

Persia was now becoming a serious threat, and in 498 BC the Ionians decided to fight for their independence.[2] They were finally defeated in c.493, but not before they had demonstrated to the Greeks that, with a unified command, resistance to Persia was not hopeless. However, the Persians, victorious against Ionia, decided to punish Athens and Eretria in Euboea which had helped it. The result was the Persian Wars. At Marathon (496), Artemisium, Salamis and Thermopylae (480), and Plataea (479), the Greeks won resounding victories. They had come together sufficiently to do so, and felt that the *ethos* of the city–states, which had united, however precariously, to win these remarkable successes but remained independent self-governing units, was justified.[3] Athens had its Delian League,[4] and Sparta remained all-powerful in the Peloponnese. But the harmony between the two powers came to an end in the late 460s, and the First, inconclusive, Peloponnesian War took place (460–445). The Athenian leader was now Pericles (495–429), who claimed that the Athenian democracy – reorganised by himself – was a model for all men. And this was the time when the culture and literature of Athens began to flourish in a manner that has never been equalled.

But then came the Second, Great Peloponnesian War (431–404), described to us with great and communicable feeling by the historian Thucydides. Athens, where Pericles died in 429, was the loser, partly because of its insane invasion of Sicily (415–413), and partly because, in the final years of the war, Persia decided to help the Spartans,[5] although this friendship did not last. The period of classical Greek supremacy was over, as the first half of the fourth century emphasised by its series of crises. Philip II of Macedon (359–336 BC) rose to power, and laid the foundations of Macedonia's greatness, although strongly opposed by the eloquent Demosthenes of Athens (384–322) (who, with Plato and Aristotle, kept the torch of Athenian cultural supremacy alive). Philip's son Alexander III the Great (d.323 BC) was a conqueror on a vast scale, and completely altered the face of the Greek world, which now entered its Hellenistic period.[6]

First of all came the age of the 'Diadochi', the successors of Alexander the Great, who divided his huge empire among themselves. But those who came after them were gradually destroyed by the rising power of Rome, which had defeated Carthage in the Second Punic War (218–204 BC). Decisive was the victory of Titus Quinctius Flamininus at Cynoscephalae (Mavrovouni) (197), which concluded the Second Macedonian War (the Third was won at Pydna [Makrygialos] twenty-nine years later), and Rome also defeated Antiochus III of Syria at Thermopylae and Magnesia (Manisa) (189), and demolished Corinth (146). In 133 Attalus III Philometor Euergetes of Pergamum (Bergama) left his kingdom to the Romans, who made it into their province of Asia. Ptolemaic Egypt (the state founded by Alexander's lieutenant Ptolemaeus I, c.367/7–283/2) was temporarily saved by Cleopatra VII (d.30), who formed liaisons with Julius Caesar and Marcus Antonius (Mark Antony); but after her death Egypt became another Roman province.

Reference has already been made to Rome's victories over Carthage and the successor-states of Alexander the Great. But it must be added that these triumphs created internal convulsions, which finally brought down the Roman Republic. This, according to tradition, had been founded towards the end of the sixth century BC; and it was certainly very ancient. As tribunes representing the sovereign authority of the Roman people Tiberius Sempronius

Gracchus (d.133) and his brother Gaius (d.122) challenged the monopoly of government by the Senate. They did not succeed, although the *equites* (knights) now emerged as a political force. But then followed the sharp confrontation between Gaius Marius and Lucius Cornelius Sulla, who became supreme dictator (82). He retired in 79, but the Republic was on its way out, despite efforts by Cicero to revive it (Lucretius and Catullus wrote their poetry at this period). Caius Julius Caesar formed the First Triumvirate (60) with Gnaeus Pompeius and Marcus Licinius Crassus, but Crassus was killed by the Parthians at Carrhae (Altibaşak),[7] and Caesar, who had annexed Gaul, defeated the Pompeians and became dictator, until he was murdered in 44, by a group led by Brutus and Cassius.[8]

After the battle of Mutina (Modena), in which the murderers of Caesar were vanquished (43), the three Caesarian leaders, Marcus Antonius (Antony), Gaius Octavius (Octavian) and Marcus Aemilius Lepidus, formed the Second Triumvirate. Lepidus retired and became High Priest (36), and Octavian defeated Antony at Actium (31), after which Antony died at Alexandria, where he had formed an association with Queen Cleopatra VII. Now Octavian, soon to be called Augustus (27 BC; d.AD 14), was the sole ruler of what had become a large empire. He also founded the Principate, an elaborate imperial system disguised beneath a constitutional framework, which his successors proceeded gradually to throw off, as is revealed by the historian Tacitus. As far as the initial (Julio-Claudian) dynasty was concerned, they were Tiberius (AD 14–37), Gaius (Caligula: 37–41), Claudius (41–54) and Nero (54–68). There followed a period of civil war, 'The Year of the Four Emperors' (AD 69), and then the Flavian dynasty which Vespasian (69–79) founded and handed on to his two sons, Titus (79–81) and Domitian (81–96).[9]

The century that followed, most of which was occupied by the so-called 'Five Good Emperors', has been hailed as the supreme and happiest epoch that the world has ever known, although the slaves were not consulted in the formation of that opinion. But it certainly was a peaceful and prosperous period. The age that followed it, centred upon the figure of Septimius Severus (193–211), was a good deal grimmer, because the army had risen to power, since it was needed as never before to cope with invasions by the Germans in the north, to whom, before long, were added on the eastern front the Persians, who had succeeded the less danger-ous Parthians (226).[10] In the Roman empire, faced with these threats, inadequate arrangements (or rather none) regarding the succession created a miserable period of military anarchy, described in this book. Historians might well have concluded that the Roman empire was at an end, but if so, as has been said, they were wrong: for a series of powerful emperors, who have been described here, pulled the empire together again, and repelled those who sought to destroy it.[11]

Then, out of a welter of short-lived rulers, emerged Diocletian, who held power for twenty-one years (284–305), revived the empire, and abdicated. Concluding that this vast territory could not be ruled by a single man, Diocletian had divided it between two Augusti, each with a Caesar to help him. Yet the arrangement broke down after his abdication, and renewed civil war followed. The ultimate victor was Constantine I the Great (306–337).[12] What Constantine did was to refound Byzantium as Constantinople, thus setting the scene for the Byzantine empire which would last for a thousand years; and he took Christianity into partnership with the State. He required national unity, but unity did not follow, since Christianity spawned heresies. Nevertheless, Constantine became sole ruler of the empire. But it was divided again when Valentinian I (364–375) gave the east to his brother Valens.

After the death of Aetius at the hands of Valentinian III (454), and the latter's consequent murder (455), the end of the western dynasty was marked by a series of brief reigns, each under the shadow of a supreme German commander, until the abdication of the last western emperor, Romulus Augustulus, in 476.[13] This event is often held to mark the end of the ancient world, which had seemed to be collapsing so much earlier. Yet it remains hard to draw a definite line between ancient times and the Middle Ages, particularly because of the survival of the eastern or Byzantine empire, with only a comparatively brief intermission, until 1453.

SOURCES

How do we learn about the ancient Greco-Roman world, which so nearly collapsed in the third century AD, and what it was like?

Well, first of all from the Greek and Roman historians themselves, among whom Herodotus, Thucydides, Polybius, Julius Caesar, Sallust and Tacitus are the most eminent and best known. And they are splendid writers, infinitely well worth reading. But they are experts of disinformation and mystification. Indeed, very often they lived long after (and in some cases far away from) the supposed 'facts' that they record: although they lived long before the period described in this book. Moreover, they concentrate on political and military affairs, so that for subjects such as slavery, the economy and women we do not find them particularly worthwhile. In order to obtain a fuller picture we must make the most extensive possible use of inscriptions and coins. Only then will we have something like an accurate idea of what was really going on: although the coins, in particular, voiced a good deal of imperial propaganda. Yet the great historians are superb writers, and very often provide us with our best, or perhaps even our only, account of what was happening.

With regard to the later Roman empire, however, which, in this respect, includes the period discussed in the present book – that is not the case. It is a very important period or series of periods, since it constitutes the bridge between the ancient and medieval worlds. But there is no first-class historian to commemorate these epochs. And for that reason they are neglected in schools and universities, which tend to prefer writers who write good, classical Latin and Greek, and do not therefore much care for those – and indeed, as has been said, they are comparatively few and unreliable – whose subject is the later Roman empire, from the third century onwards.

OUR HERITAGE

My first reaction, on hearing someone question whether a knowledge of the Greco-Roman classics is important to us, is to reply that he or she need their heads seeing to. However, on reflection, it becomes clear that this is not an adequate answer: the reasons why the classics are important to us do have to be explained. For one thing, people cannot adequately face the problems of the present and the future without understanding the past that has bred us. It is acutely, even at times painfully, relevant to the experiences that we ourselves have to face.

The classics consist of Greece and of Rome. Of course, there were other ancient civilisations as well, and Greece and Rome owed a lot to them. But that does not prevent Greece and Rome from being highly individual. Rome owed a great deal to Greece. Yet, all the same, the Roman achievement was very different, and again highly individual. We are entitled, and rightly so, to speak of a single Greco-Roman civilisation, which very

Figure 24 Coin of Ardashir (Artaxerxes I) (© British Museum).

Figure 25 Coin of Sapor I (© British Museum).

Figure 26 Coin of Sol. (Photograph courtesy of Michael Grant).

nearly, but not quite, came to an end in the epoch discussed in this book. But let us not forget the Greek heritage when we do speak accordingly we must remember how very different the two parts of this, to us, cohesive entity were.

On this whole question of the greatness, and importance to us, of Greece and Rome, let me quote a few estimates:

> To forget the value of the inheritance which Rome pre-
> served for us . . . is merely a passing phase of feeling: it is
> really quite inconsistent with the character of an age which

recognises the doctrine of evolution as its great discovery. It is natural for civilised man to go back upon his past, and to be grateful for all profit he can gain from the study of his own development.

So we may be certain that the claim of Greece and Rome to our eternal gratitude, will never cease to be asserted, and their right to teach us still what we could have learnt somewhere else, will never be successfully disputed.[14]

Our modern world is in many ways a continuation of the world of Greece and Rome. Not in all ways – particularly not in medicine, music, industry and applied science. But in most of our intellectual and spiritual activities we are the grandsons of the Romans, and the great-grandsons of the Greeks. Other influences joined to make us what we are; but the Greco-Roman strain was one of the strongest and richest.

Without it, our civilisation would not merely be different. It would be much thinner, more fragmentary, less thoughtful, more materialistic. . . . In civilisation as in human life, the present is the child of the past.[15]

It is an axiom of history that the basic ideas and expressions of the European way of life are derived organically from those shaped by Athens in the sixth and fifth centuries BC. The miracle continues to produce a tireless literature but is happily one that defies ultimate analysis. . . . [Athens] was always poor enough to challenge the enterprise of its inhabitants, [but] is the primary citadel of Europe.[16]

In other words, everything goes back to the Greeks. We are all Greeks. We are the inheritors of their virtues and vices – their fierce competitive spirit, their intellectual curiosity, their will to action. It is this heritage which defines us, makes us a people different from those who have grown up in the religious faiths and philosophies of the East: it is, for better or worse, the driving force of that civilisation we call western.[17]

And I myself have said the following about this, stressing that one must pay attention to the Romans as well as the Greeks.

The classics form a large part of the basis of our own civilisation. Without them, there would be no civilisation, as we understand the term. And the classical element is not just Greek culture, but what the Romans made of it. So Gladstone's view that the tremendous greatness of Greece makes Rome unimportant is obsolete. The fact that Rome was preceded by the Greeks is no reason why it should be ignored or underrated. . . .

There is need of people who, with admiration for the achievements of previous scholars but without automatic acceptance of everything they have said, will attack the engrossing problems. . . . The quest is worthwhile, since its reward is that enriched knowledge of part thought which can help us to face the future with experience, and so with a measure of confidence. . . .

We ourselves, whether we like it or not, are the heirs of the Greeks and Romans. . . . Without that massive contribution we should not be what we are. Its influences crowd in upon us insistently from many sides, having reached us in numerous different ways, and at every level of consciousness and profundity. The Greeks and Romans lived through a variety of events and developments – political, social, literary, artistic – which prefigured and prompted what has subsequently happened, what is still happening, and what will happen in the future, to our own lives and our own communities.

Circumstances and backgrounds, of course, have come to differ radically over the centuries. Yet to be able to see no relevant lessons or warnings in this Greco-Roman world would be strangely mistaken. For it is a world that can show us the good and bad things of which humanity has been capable, and may therefore be capable of again. . . . Without awareness of this background we are blindfolded in our efforts to grapple with this future.[18]

The worst sufferers from this current decline have been the languages, Latin and Greek. It is an English myth that one has to learn Latin in one's childhood. When I was in the United States, many of my students only began to learn Latin after they had gone to university, and by the time they graduated they were quite good. We ought to know some Latin. Its current decline, in our own century as in many others, is unfortunate, for a variety of reasons. But we must not ignore translations.

The Greek had excelled in [poetry]. Yet, on occasion, Roman poetry is unsurpassed and unsurpassable in the subtlety of its sound-effects and the satisfying quality of its rhythm, in its expressive and musical terseness. Roman literature, then, had a vigorous life and character of its own. So it is wrong to think of it only in the somewhat humble role of transmitter. This was a mistake often made in the nineteenth century. . . . [But] Latin writers . . . added a highly individual series of contributions of their own. . . . 'The Latin mind, as it expressed and recorded itself in Latin literature, was not only transforming, but constructive and creative.

Without Latin, neither the English language nor the literature which is the greatest glory of the English-speaking race would be what they are.[19]

In the nineteenth century, authors assumed that the greater part of the literature of the Western world was produced by men who were familiar with the Greek tradition, either directly or through the medium of Latin; who were conscious that the forms they used were mostly of Greek invention and who took for granted in their readers some familiarity with classical literature.[20] The merits and demerits of translating this literature have often been discussed.

Greek and Latin literature continued: let us not fall into the trap of thinking that it ended with Ovid, or even with Tacitus. In other words, we should remember – and as moderns it is not difficult for us to do so – that the inhabitants of the Roman empire during the second century AD read novels. For example, they read Apuleius (in Latin) and Longus (in Greek), and, as we have seen, in the third century, they read Heliodorus.

As regards the law, most of us are not solicitors or barristers. Yet even if we are not, it is worth remembering that the entire world of order, in which we live, is the creation of the ancients, and in particular of the Romans. It is true that the law of our land, as we know it today, is not Roman Law. Nevertheless, it was the Romans, after various more or less localised Greek efforts, who concluded that we ought to live within a legal framework. And that is what we do. In other words, we live our lives through the grace of Roman Law. So we owe it to the Roman lawyers – and to Cicero who interpreted so much of what they said – that we live in comparative peace and orderliness. Without Roman Law, we should merely be in the jungle.

It is very difficult, however, to advise the classical student what to read about Roman Law, because one can hardly expect him or her to study the works of the great jurists, Quintus Mucius Scaevola during the Republic, Javolenus Priscus during the early second century AD, Salvius Julianus (c.AD 100–c.169) and Sextus Pomponius of about the same date, Quintus Cervidius Scaevola during the later second century AD, and Papinian, Paulus and Ulpian under the dynasty of the Severans (AD 193–235); although the existence of the last named does remind us, as teachers do not always, that Roman history does not come to a halt before the time of Cicero and Caesar.

One might have thought that, in view of the unmistakable and logical importance of the classics, they would flourish today. But they do not. They are declining.[21] And ancient historians, as we have seen, although some of them were brilliant writers, do not always succeed in bringing that world before us, being uninterested, for example – as we have seen – in slavery, the economy, women and homosexuals. Here I would fasten particularly upon two themes concerning which we have a great deal to learn from the ancient world, although the first of them, at least, only achieved verbal praise during the period described in this book.

First, democracy. When politicians use the word so glibly – although little is heard of it in the epochs I have just mentioned – have we any idea what they mean? As a first stage, let us compare and contrast the representative democracy that we have today (although it is compromised and undermined by the repeated call for referenda, which pay no attention to our representatives) with the direct democracy of ancient Athens (limited, in practice, by the exclusion of women and slaves). It seems to me that when modern politicians use this ancient term they do so in order to contrast our own 'democratic' order with the dictatorships that exist elsewhere; and to make such a contrast is entirely legitimate – and, incidentally, does owe something to our incorporation of the ancient world into our systems of government. However, it does not do to forget what democracy really means and how it came into being.

This was Stobart's comment on Greek political activity:

> They met with disastrous failures which are full of teaching for us. . . . For us, an imperial people, who have inherited a vast and scattered dominion which somehow or other has got to be managed and governed, the chief interest will

centre in the question of how these city–states acquired and administered their empires. Above all it is to Athens and perhaps Rome alone that we can look for historical answers to the great riddle for which we cannot yet boast of having discovered a solution – whether democracy can govern an empire. . . . We [also] have a momentous phase of the eternal and still-continuing conflict between East and West and their respective habits of civilisation. . . .

Whosoever from the beginning of his action already contemplates its final end and adapts his means thereto in earnest simplicity, whoever knows that pride and vain ostentation will assuredly bring its own punishment, of whatever land or age he may be, he is a Greek. In that sense we cannot close Greek history.[22]

A major debt which the history of the Greco-Roman world has bestowed upon us is provided by the Roman empire, about which the present book has a lot to say. Quite apart from the intrinsic interest, not to say excitement, provided by the sight of all this history, over many centuries, being laid before us – including the virtual collapse of the empire in the later third century – it is impossible not to find this tale relevant to what had happened, and is happening, in modern times. Those of us who are old enough have seen the British empire intact and in action; and many who are younger have witnessed the conduct and operation of the Soviet Empire. French, Italians and Germans also have recent experiences of their own to meditate upon. And now, as we know, there is a great move to establish a united Europe. It will not have quite the same boundaries as the ancient Roman empire, but it is impossible not to see that empire as a sort of forerunner. (Unlike the Roman empire, we hope it will not be established by force.) For this reason alone it is desirable to study Greece and Rome: they established, over a vast area, the unity that we are trying to establish today. They did so partly by force: but having used force they then proceeded to offer reasonably fair administration.

Here are a few modern comments on the Roman empire:

Seldom has the government of the world been conducted for so long a term in an orderly sequence. . . . In its sphere, which those who belonged to it were not far wrong in regarding as the world, it fostered the peace and prosperity of the many nations united under its sway longer and more completely than any other leading power has ever done. . . .

If an angel of the Lord were to strike the balance whether the domain ruled by Severus Alexander [AD 222–235] were governed with the greater intelligence and the greater humanity at that time or at the present day, whether civilisation and national prosperity have since that time advanced or retrograded, it is very doubtful whether the decision would prove in favour of the present.

Geographically, the Roman empire stretched, at its peak, three thousand miles from southern Scotland to southern Egypt; on the east, Roman frontiers lay in the sun-baked upper plains along the Euphrates River, and on the west stopped only at the Atlantic Ocean. This huge block was larger than the whole earth today, if measured in terms of ancient communications and transportation. . . .

Modern historians have great difficulty in describing the Roman empire both in time and space. . . . Overall the political, economic and military structure of the empire was one of the most successful in human history in giving centuries of stability and order.[23]

Of course one reason why we may not be all that attached to Greece and Rome is because theirs was primarily a Mediterranean civilisation, whereas our own is not. That is true enough, but it does not alter the fact, already stated, that we have inherited a great deal from that culture, and have a lot to learn from it. Furthermore, it extended a great deal north of the Mediterranean, indeed to our own shores. And, in any case, the Roman world provides us with valuable lessons about how a multinational state should be organised and governed.

RELIGIONS

We must not forget ancient religion. However, we are rather up against it when we come to consider the subject. For the fact is that the Greeks and Romans were religious peoples: they believed that whatever happened, and whatever they did, was conditioned by the will of the gods, or of God. This attitude is manifest from Homer onwards. On the other hand, we moderns do not live in very religious societies. There are occasional *gurus*, who with their supporters whip up allegedly religious thinking. But, first of all, they are, as has been said, only occasional and, second, they do not belong to the mainstream of Christian tradition. Apart from them, religion is not strong today. Ask the Church of England, or any other official religious body. How many people understand the doctrine of the Trinity? Do you?

Yet because the Greeks and Romans, on the contrary, were so deeply religious, it is not possible to comprehend them or their history or literatures without knowing something about their religion, alien though it may seem to us. First of all, there is the polytheistic religion of Greek and Roman paganism. We must recognise what this had to offer, and not, as is much more customary, reject it out of hand. Perhaps one of the most significant aspects of this polytheistic paganism is the Parthenon at Athens. But paganism was also greatly developed by the Romans; and, for example, the imperial cult needs to be considered.

However, let us also consider the Jews, whose religion had been in existence for a long time, and the Christians, who replaced the Roman pagans. It is noteworthy, one must repeat, that one is able to find people today who profess to be Jews or Christians but show not the slightest knowledge of how their religions came into existence or developed. The Bible, in other words, needs the historian, and (in the case of the New Testament) the classicist to explain it.

Christians, Jews, agnostics and atheists must be equally concerned with the rise of monotheism in the Greek and Roman world, where it gradually replaced polytheism: as certain examples quoted in this book have shown. That is to say, it was a development from paganism, and how it developed is a matter of absorbing interest. So it is the extraordinary replacement of paganism by Christianity under Constantine the Great and some of his successors, this being one of the systems that offered relief from an aimless and comfortless world. Nor do the great Christian writers receive enough attention from most of those who teach the Classics. One of them was St Augustine. Another was Jerome.

If we view sanctity in the guise of beatified sweetness – as was the fashion during a large part of the nineteenth century – then we must confess that Jerome would not figure in the establishment. But the folk of the Middle Ages and the epoch that succeeded them liked their saints to be tough. And Jerome, the darling of Roman drawing-rooms, the scintillating talker and scholar, who might have been excused for being a smooth man, he it was who was to prove himself as hardy as the sons of thunder, and to take the kingdom of heaven, as it were, by storm.

For Rome, by this time, was no longer entirely, or even mainly, a pagan society. But that does not mean that paganism has to be ignored, either at Rome – even during the epochs discussed in this book – or, earlier, in the period when the ancient Greek city–states were independent. Instead, the origins of Greek paganism and polytheism are a fascinating subject, which has frequently been dealt with.

Christian pilgrimage was also a very important factor in the later Roman empire.

To sum up, early Christianity, like the paganism that preceded it, is a phenomenon which we have to consider if we are to have any understanding of what the ancient world was all about. Yes, that world was a lot more religious than we mostly are. Therefore we must study its religious attitudes in order to find out what was happening.

ARCHAEOLOGY AND ARCHITECTURE

We will find that the archaeology, which so greatly helps an under-standing of the ancient world, is changing shape very rapidly. With the aid of modern technological devices, including properly equipped aeroplanes, the epoch of the traditional 'digger' is nearly at an end. Indeed, in the future, digging itself may be regarded as hardly necessary. And yet the sites that have been described here could not have been revealed without digging, which will surely remain a key feature of archaeology.

At Athens, of course, it is desirable to see the Acropolis, and to visit the Parthenon and Erechtheum which stand there, and to learn from them – or from other temples, because they are numerous – what the Greeks made of the temple architecture that they created.[24]

In a way, architecture is the easiest and most obvious approach to the Greek and Roman worlds, since one can see so many of the surviving relics still in existence (often from periods preceding those described in the present book). The remains of Athens, Rome, Pompeii, etc., are more illuminating to most people than any of the literary survivals mentioned above. In Britain, too, there are valuable and revealing sites. As for Greek architecture, to many people this means temples.

The mental picture formed at the sound of the words 'Greek architecture' is likely to be that of a temple or part of a temple, and of a Doric one at that. Nor would this be unfair to the fact that we are in a position to study the remains of a great variety of ancient Greek buildings. Though no city in classical times was deemed complete without its *agora* or 'city-centre', round which stood the public buildings, colonnaded shops, lawcourts, as well as theatre, gymnasium, stadium, fountain-houses, monuments to its heroes and of course its defensible acropolis, it was commonly the temple of the city's patron god or goddess which was given the dominant position and the highest honour.

Is such an architecture, which continued throughout the Roman empire, an art? Obviously it is, and the ancients believed that this was so: not only the Greeks, but the Romans as well, who have likewise left us remarkable architectural evidence of themselves.

At the very same time as Fishbourne was created in Britain, the emperor Vespasian (AD 69–79) founded the greatest of all amphitheatres at Rome – which was still in existence when the period discussed in this book began and ended. We have every reason to dislike the gladiatorial combats and animal fights for which it was created, but there is no doubt – and here there is a curious paradox – about the architectural masterpieces which were their product. And then came the Pantheon of Hadrian (117–138), which is one of the greatest buildings of all time.

But it would be a serious mistake not to include Africa and Asia Minor and Syria among the regions where the Romans created magnificent architecture. For example, Septimius Severus (193–211), shortly before our period, created a new Forum at his birth-place Lepcis Magna (Lebda) in Tripolitana (North Africa), a modified and improved version of the famous Forum Romanum at the capital.

The late Romans were also attentive to the near east, where there were mighty temples not only at Palmyra (Tadmor) but also at Heliopolis (Baalbek) in Syria, created by a judicious blend of Roman, Greek and eastern influences.

In the splendid ruins of Heliopolis and Palmyra we can see a riotous luxuriance of ornament which would have shocked the religious sense of fifth-century BC architects, but which aptly enshrined the ritual and mysteries of the Sun-god. This craze for the colossal would have made the reverential Greeks tremble in fear of provoking the Nemesis of a jealous Heaven, but its ruins have left us superb and awful reminders of the riches and grandeurs of its authors.

The early Christians continued and developed the old tradition of fine architecture in the near East, and particular attention needs to be focused on Qal'at Sem'an in Syria. The immense reputation of St Simeon made Qal'at Sem'an a major centre of pilgrimage, which was very fashionable in the fifth centuy, being encouraged (as far as Rome was concerned) by Pope Leo I the Great.

Mention must also be made of the immense Roman interest in bathing. Bath-buildings were normally combined with libraries, lecture-halls, lounges, sport-grounds and gardens. The climax was provided by the Baths of Caracalla and Diocletian.

Nor was bathing the only concern of imperial Roman architects; for they also built great aqueducts. In a sense, this was linked with the national love of bathing, because it provided the water that made the great Baths possible; and this predilection continued during the eras that are here under discussion. Triumphal arches and massive walls were also an important part of Roman architecture; and they reached a climax during the later empire. They played no functional role, but were a perpetual reminder of the power and grandeur of Rome and its empire.

And let us conclude with Pompeii, which, together with Herculaneum and Stabiae, revealed all the main features that made buildings such a prominent Roman art; although they themselves had been destroyed long before the period described in this book.[25]

At a much later date (even after the period that is the subject of the present volume), the walls of Constantinople demand special mention.

> The Inner, or Great, Wall was the main defence. . . . It is thirty to forty feet high, and fourteen to fifteen feet thick. . . . Its ninety-six towers are about sixty feet high and of all shapes, from square to octagonal. . . .
>
> Between this Great Wall and the outer wall is an inner terrace (*peribolus*), sixty feet wide. The outer wall is from three to six feet thick, and about thirty feet high. The lower part forms a retaining wall for the inner terrace, the upper is an arcade, with a rampart over barrel vaults. Its towers rise about thirty feet above the terrace, and are alternately square or crescent; variations upon these forms being the

result of hurried repairs. Beyond the outer wall, again, is the outer terrace, sixty feet high, and sheltered from the moat by a battlement six feet high. . . . The moat is also sixty feet wide, and was probably at least thirty feet deep. . . . The Gates are alternately Military and Public; the former admitting only to the fortifications, the latter to the city highways. . . . Originally the Theodosian Walls continued along their own line across to the Golden Horn.[26]

ART AND SCULPTURE

The Greek and Roman world made enormous advances in the field of sculpture, and their advances, which are very conspicuous in the later third century AD, are still with us today. That is to say, our modern sculpture, such as it is, owes a great deal to the ancients, and that is true even of the sculptors who are consciously in revolt against them. And this ancient contribution forms a substantial part of the achievement of the ancient world, and of the period discussed in this book.

Probably some people today may not like ancient sculpture, because they will regard it as a relativist taste, which served the wishes of the rich. But:

> Greek sculpture has its roots in the religious and political life of the people. The work of the sculptor gave form to gods conceived in human image and adorned their temples and sanctuaries; it celebrated political events, honoured athletic victories, commemorated the dead.
>
> Of all the arts, sculpture best expresses the genius of the Greek people, and in the fifth century it achieved an ideal of human form, grounded in nature but rising far above it, that is one of their greatest legacies. . . . The Greeks loved colour and, rather surprisingly to us, they painted their marble statuary and architecture in bright colours. . . . Although much Greek sculpture has survived, most of the great masterpieces have gone long since into the melting-pot or the lime-kiln, but . . . the sculpture from dated buildings provides a firm chronological sequence of the development of the art.[27]

What is mainly wrong about this attitude is to suppose that art has no unchangeable standards. For it has. Some art is good, and some is bad. And it was the Greeks, and then the Romans, who taught us to distinguish between the two.

It is hardly surprising that the Greeks were good at sculpture, because whatever their faults, they knew how to sculpt: and they infused into their products a truly artistic and intellectual force, which was not altogether lost in even quite late imperial Roman times.

Sculpture may be divided into two halves: sculpture in the round, and sculpture in relief. In both the Greeks and Romans were very good. To consider sculpture in the round first, the Athenians led the way when they commissioned statues of the tyrant-slayers Harmodius and Aristogeiton. The originals have not survived, but the enterprise was important as a forerunner of what the Romans were able to achieve.

When we come to the greatest sculptors of the fifth century BC, including Phidias, let us this time ignore what has gone, and concentrate on the sculptures in the round that have survived, so that what remains of them can still be seen, and could be seen during the period with which this book is concerned. Into this category fall the figures that were upon the pediment of the Parthenon on the Acropolis at Athens, and are now in the British Museum.

After the Parthenon, there were three great fourth-century sculptors – Praxiteles, Scopas, Lysippus. These three sculptors gave to Greek art a new direction, which the Romans attempted to follow. And then came the Hellenistic age, which brought much increased realism. Indeed, where the Greco-Roman period really excelled was portraiture – which gives the lie to the assumption that architecture was the only art in which the Romans were conspicuous: and this excellence of portraiture is particularly to be noted in the epoch to which this book is devoted.

But, first, we must consider the Greek achievement in this field. As the portraits of Pericles and Alexander III the Great show, the Greeks were principally concerned to delineate ideal beauty in human shape: but it is a clear indication of the future that they devoted so much care to the portrayal of leading men.

By the time of the emperors, a considerable, sophisisticated, tradition of Roman portraiture already existed.[28] And of this the emperors made the fullest use, in relation to themselves, for propagandist purposes. Their imperial busts were made, or circulated, all over the empire. The emperor was represented as

Figure 27 Unknown woman. (Museo Vaticano, Rome. Archivio Fotografico, Monumenti Musei e Gallerie Pontificie).

man of religion, as democratic statesman, as Greek thinker or hero–god, as world conqueror.

The custom of imperial busts continued, and indeed it might be said that it reached its climax in the third century AD, with a bust first of Caracalla (211–217), and then of Philip the Arab (244–249), in the Vatican, discussed in this book.

Not long afterwards the long-standing tradition of realistic busts came to an end, because, for example, the colossal head of Constantine I the Great (306–337), in the courtyard of the Conservatori Museum at Rome, is far more hieratic and impersonal.[32]

But what a history imperial portraiture had had! It is difficult to understand the ancient world, or at least the latter part of it, including the epoch discussed in this book, without knowing something about these portraits.

And no one will be in a position to appreciate the ancient Greco-Roman civilisation unless he or she realises that it expressed itself partly by sculptures in relief. These partook of the qualities already ascribed to sculptures in the round, but they also had a good deal to add. Once again, we have to be selective, since there are so many examples one could quote, although the result of including so much material would inevitably be chaotic.

But let us once again go back to Athens, and to the Parthenon upon the Acropolis – about which we shall all be hearing more, because the Greeks claim the sculptures back from the British Museum. The Parthenon not only displayed sculptural figures in the round on the pediments, which have been discussed, but very important relief sculptures in the metopes[29] round the temple, and in the frieze that extended all round the *cella*. The metopes have frequently been discussed.

And then we come to the Parthenon frieze, in the British Museum, is about 160 metres long. It depicts the annual festival of the Panathenata, in which, every fourth year, a new robe (*peplos*) was taken in procession to the Acropolis.[30]

The Romans, of all periods, fully understood the importance of relief sculpture, and their régime greatly developed it as one of the principal means of self-expression and propaganda.

The language is already visible in the reliefs of Augustus's Ara Pacis (Altar of Peace) at Rome, but reaches its climax on the winding surfaces of the great columns of Trajan (AD 98–117) and Marcus Aurelius (161–180) in the same city, while both were still standing (the former is still) during the period described in this book.

> [the reliefs on Trajan's Column] are, above all, a magnificent commemoration of the Roman army's achievements, with the emperor as comrade and leader: they are essentially an

epic of all members, in all capacities, of the imperial forces – the most impressive armed forces put into the field until recent times.[31]

What is particularly interesting, however, and valuable to those who wish to see what the Roman empire was like, is to note that far away from Rome local artists, with their own styles, embraced similar propagandist conceptions.

Just occasionally works of art in the Roman provinces seem quite uninfluenced by the pervasive Greco-Roman traditions. One such example is provided by the reliefs on the Trophy of Trajan (Tropaeum Trajani) at Adamklissi – although the theme is entirely imperial: the victory of Trajan over the Dacians, whose country he annexed early in the second century AD. The victory was celebrated by thoroughly Greco-Roman reliefs on the Column of Trajan at Rome. But at Adamklissi a Dacian sculptor or sculptors brought to the task a strong measure of local taste and talent, producing masterpieces which are out of keeping with the dominant classical styles.

Triumphal arches, as we have seen, were another means the rulers used to commemorate the greatness of their empire. There are several examples at Rome itself, including one of Septimius Severus (193–211), but especial attention should be paid by those who are concerned with sculpture or relief to the great four-way Arch of Septimius Severus at Lepcis Magna in Tripolitania, which is one of many in Severan Africa.

There is a kind of incorporeal illusionism, an exploration of impressionistic, dematerialised, optical effects, a rhythmical, repetitive symmetry. The sculptors are Asian, and there is also evidence of African influence.[32]

Another form of Roman artistic development, without a knowledge of which it is impossible to understand what was going on in the empire, was the sarcophagus. What started this fashion was the gradual replacement of cremation by inhumation in the second century AD.

The mosaic is also of great importance. The Greeks who invented mosaic decoration used black and white pebbles in their natural rounded state. Hitherto very few such pebble mosaics had been known, but the first house excavated at Pella produced three of them, excellent in composition and full of spirited movement. Dionysus rides his bounding panther; a griffin attacks a fleeing deer, and two men with sword and spear engage a lion. The latest archaeological report mentions the discovery of four more mosaics in another house.

Then, in Hellenistic times, pebbles were replaced by more colourful *tesserae*; as recent finds at Morgantina (in Sicily) have confirmed. These floor mosaics have survived because, owing to their materials, they are better equipped to do so than, say, the paintings which they often copy.

At Pompeii there are already a few mosaics on walls and ceilings rather than floors. And then, in the Roman world that became Christian, mosaics crept up from floors altogether, on to the walls and apses of churches. Rome is full of examples of the new sort of mosaic on the walls and apses of churches, and it is essential also to remember that they were to be found all over the eastern (Byzantine) empire as well. Asia Minor is very notable in this respect, especially in the late Roman period, for example, the mosaic in the church at Elaeusa (Ayaş) is noteworthy.

There are three types of ancient Greek and Roman painting with which we ought to familiarise ourselves if we are to understand how people lived and what they thought in the Greco-Roman world. They are Greek 'vase'-painting, the wall-paintings of Pompeii, and neighbouring towns, and Romano-Egyptian mummy portraits.

'Vase' painting, the painting of pottery, was of course one of the principal Greek arts, from quite an early date. The Athenians made great claims for their painting; and they probably exaggerated, although they were certainly the leaders.

Critias, the late fifth-century Athenian poet and politician, claimed that it was Athens 'that invented the potter's wheel and the offspring of clay and kiln, pottery so famous and useful about the house'. Although this claim is probably not true, Athenian clay was one of the finest Greek clays by reason of its excellent working characteristics and its warm orange-red colour, and it was at Athens that the art of pottery reached its peak.

There was also a lot of Roman painting, learnt, originally, when Roman Italy was flooded with Greek originals from the early third century BC onwards. The student can learn best about what was achieved – and what, after all, constituted one of the main features of the Roman civilisation – from Pompeii, Herculaneum and Stabiae. There we see the evolution of an art-form of paramount importance in the ancient world: the interior decoration of the Roman villa. To which I myself added that:

Wall paintings . . . constitute, all in all, the most remarkable aspect of Pompeii and Herculaneum. . . . These paintings provide a vivid reflection of daily life in ancient times; through them, we gain insight into the aesthetic experience of Rome and are able to see which themes were considered important in Roman society. . . . They were part of a life-style.[33]

Some of these paintings are, as one might expect, mediocre, but *The Lost Ram*, apparently of the Fourth Style though we do not know to which room of a villa it belonged, is a masterpiece, as I have tried to explain elsewhere.[34]

Mummy portraits are also of considerable significance, particularly when we recall that many of them were still being made during the period described in this volume.

The other truly important movement in the paintings of the Roman empire is that of the mummy-'portrait' artists in Egypt, whose work ranges in date from the early first century BC until the fourth century AD. . . . These 'portraits' replaced, to a large extent, the plaster-masks that had been used in Hellenistic Egypt. What makes them notable is their artists' capacity to display what seem to be the characters of the men and women (prominent here) whose dead bodies are mummified. . . . They are lifelike images. They make us delight in the people represented. . . . Yet one wonders whether these heads are *really* portraits: or are they, despite their vividness, somewhat standard images of the dead? Or had they been, after all, made while the subjects were alive – but still presumably not from personal portrayal? Whatever the answers to these questions, the heads are meant to be images of people who will be resurrected for eternity. . . .

[Their] colours possess a special, rich and brilliant quality, which seems a little garish at times – but often looks like a forecast of modern oil painting. . . . These heads . . . make a remarkable impact, not only because they seem to anticipate our own age, but because, despite the queries relating to generalisation raised above, their human interest is so strong. In the best of these 'portraits', or 'heads' as we had better call them, the countenances are captivatingly depicted, the highlighted drawing is sharp and graceful, and the general level of craftsmanship is high. . . .

There seems to have been a double tradition, of Roma-
nised Hellenism and Egyptian Pharaonic Art.

From a very early date the governments of the Greek city–states,
and then later of the Roman Republic and Empire, made ample use
of their coinage for propaganda purposes and in order to explain
what they were trying to do (cf. Chapter 7): and this activity was
still extremely noticeable in the period discussed in this book.

> In order to interpret the significance of ancient coins, we
> have to forget many features of our modern currency. The
> passage of two thousand years has changed our ideas about
> many things, and coinage is one of them. . . . No modern
> dictator distributes his portraits so thoroughly as the Roman
> Fathers 'of the Country' circulated theirs. . . . [And] it is
> with news that the reverses are crammed. . . . Roman coin-
> age . . . was intended to be looked at, and was looked at.[35]

This remarkable activity was initiated and developed by Greece and
Rome, whose civilisation so nearly, but not quite, collapsed during
this period.

The Classics, then, should be looked at, because this is a study
which is infinitely worthwhile, which provides a suitable guide to
living, and which, by telling of the past, shows us what we have to
do in the present and the future. It is not, of course, indispensable.
For example, many Swedes get on perfectly well without it. My
wife, who is Swedish, never learnt anything about the Classics at
school, and yet she is an extremely intelligent woman, with an
excellent judgement. But how much better equipped even the
Swedes would be to cope with their lives if they knew something
about the Classical past: as, indeed, a number of them do.

May I add a small piece of autobiographical information. At the
age of 51 I resigned from a very interesting university post in order
to devote myself, whole time, to writing about the Classics. And I
have never regretted it. It is an inexhaustible theme, and I have
tried to outline in this Appendix some of the many reasons why it
is worthwhile to concentrate on the Classics. The book as a whole,
however, deals with the period when the Roman empire seemed to
be breaking down, but miraculously recovered.

NOTES

INTRODUCTION

1 These fifty years have been described as the lowest point in the Roman empire, when it barely escaped complete disruption. There was a political, military, financial crisis. But there is an extraordinary lack of good contemporary literary sources, or of any ancient literary sources at all. See, in particular, A. Alföldi, *Geschichte der Weltkrise des dritten Jahrhunderts* (1967), J.N. Claster, *The Medieval Experience: AD 300–400* (1982), J.B. Griard, Gordianus III – Quintillus, G.C. Brower, *The Decadent Emperors: Power and Depravity in Third Century Rome* (1995), and, above all, E. Gibbon, *The Decline and Fall of the Roman Empire* (1766–1788; and recent editions, notably by the Readers' Subscription, and Folio Society, 1997).

1 THE SUCCESSION OF EMPERORS

1 The emperors themselves mostly came nowadays from the army, and were of humble origin. The army, however, was unreliable and so was the Roman mob.

2 J.F. Drinkwater, *Oxford Classical Dictionary*, 3rd edn, 1996, p. 787. Maximinus I Thrax probably came from a Moesian village. His father Micea was a Goth, his mother Ababa an Alan. He knew no Greek. Before his accession, he was in charge of the Rhine recruits: not commander of the *whole* army, as *Historia Augusta* (*The Two Maximinuses*, 7.1). He was the first example of a new type of ruler. On coming to the imperial throne, he almost immediately doubled army pay. Then he proceeded against the Goths and Carpi.

The Severan army is the army as reconstituted by the emperor Septimius Severus (193–211). Equestrian = knight. See also G.C. Brauer, *The Age of the Soldier-Emperors: Imperial Rome AD 244–284* (1978).

3 J.F. Drinkwater, op. cit., p. 642. Some believed that the death of Gordianus III was due to treachery by Philip. But the official story was that he had died of wounds after an eastern battle (at Misiche).

4 H.M.D. Parker, *Oxford Classical Dictionary*, 3rd edn, 1996, pp. 270ff.

5 J.F. Drinkwater, op. cit., p. 642. Ctesiphon (Taysafun) was the Persian capital. For the 'Severan monarchy' cf. note 2 above.

6 J.F. Dobson, *Oxford Classical Dictionary*, 3rd edn, 1996, p. 986. Philip's peace with the Persians has often been regarded as disgraceful.

7 B.H. Warmington and J.F. Drinkwater, ibid., p. 965. Decius had marched on Italy in 249, leaving the imperial frontiers dangerously exposed. Before Abrittus, he had been involved in heavy fighting round Philippopolis (Plovdiv), which, he hoped in vain, had left the Goths too exhausted to go on.

8 J.F. Drinkwater, op. cit., p. 1597.

9 J.F. Drinkwater, ibid., p. 19. Aemilian came from north Africa.

10 J.F. Drinkwater, ibid., p. 3860. For Sapor (Shahpur) I see also Chapter 3.

11 There were not 'Twenty' or 'Thirty' usurpers as our ancient sources insisted, but at least seven or eight. The best known are Aureolus (265) and Postumus and his successors – there is a fine array of the coins of Postumus in Auction 41 of the Cloisten Group, Lancaster, Pennsylvania, p. 232f. – and Ingenuus, and the Macriani and Quietus. Another was Uranius Antoninus, C.H.V. Sutherland, *Roman Coins* (1976), p. 232f. For the British usurpers see P.J. Casey, *Carausius and Allectas* (1994). Emperors sought to establish dynasties, honouring imperial ladies and princes.

12 The wealth of Palmyra was based on the silk trade. But the city was squeezed and perhaps over-taxed, having the difficult task of maintaining a balance between the two great powers. A wall-painting of the Palmyrene gods has been found at Dura-Europus.

13 J.F. Dobson, *Oxford Classical Dictionary*, op. cit., p. 1390.

14 The family of Odaenathus had been dominant in Palmyrene civic institutions since the 250s.

15 It is doubtful whether Odaenathus actually held this rank. Praised for the bravery and majesty, he has been said to have had, as his main purpose, the protection of his city's trade (see note 12 above).

16 While he was leader of the Roman army in the east (262–267), Odaenathus cleared Mesopotamia and Syria of Persians (though he had first wanted friendship with the Persians; and he did not succeed in capturing Ctesiphon (Taysafun). He also checked the Gothic invasion of northern Asia Minor.

17 A. Alföldi, *Cambridge Ancient History*, vol. XII (1956), b. 175. Odaenathus never claimed, or was given, the title of joint Augustus.

18 J.F. Dobson, op. cit., p. 1635.

19 Some ascribe these events to a later date. A.H.M. Jones, *Oxford Classical Dictionary*, 2nd edn. (1920), pp. 1145ff. The expedition of Heraclianus has been doubted.

2 THE GERMANS

1 For this chapter special acknowledgements are due to L. Musset, *The Germanic Invasions* (1965, 1975), J.D. Randers-Pehrson, *Barbarians and*

Romans (1983), F. Owen, *The Germanic Peoples* (1990), and M. Todd, *The Early Germans* (1992).

2 A. Bursche, *Antiquaries' Journal*, LXXVI, 1996, p. 33 (cf. the reference). There has, however, been a good deal of speculation about *why*, in the third century, the Germans became a particularly serious threat to the Roman empire.

3 The northern frontier has been described as one of the most temporary and unstable of Roman frontiers, as had already been apparent in the time of Marcus Aurelius (161–180). But Maximinus I Thrax, for all his attacks on Germany, was perhaps unwilling to make it into a Roman province; the barbarians in the army were sad about his death.

It must also be pointed out that the Germans who nowadays formed a prominent part of the Roman army (M. Todd, op. cit., p. 59), had assimilated Roman military and other techniques (including education), but that Rome was glad to exploit the lack of unified purpose among them, and kept the peace, for a time, by the payment of subsidies, which the Germans (being short of gold, silver and iron) were happy to extort. Nevertheless, there was a series of struggles, in which – as the coinage was eager to proclaim – the Romans won military 'victories', driving the Germans back into their forests, although failing, in spite of these successes, to put an end to the German threat. L. Musset, op. cit., p. 15, sums up the situation:

> There was an obvious gulf between the Germanic world and Roman society: the former inspired by an extraordinary dynamism but completely rural, almost illiterate, without any real political organisation; the latter somewhat decaying, based on . . . written laws . . . and the crushing authority of a totalitarian bureaucracy.

4 J.F. Drinkwater, *Oxford Classical Dictionary*, 3rd edn (1996), p. 49. For Aurelian, see below, Chapter 4. The Alamanni seem to have undertaken a powerful regrouping in *c.*200, and, although their loose confederation did not yet form distinct political centres, they violently attacked the Roman empire from *c.*231, or earlier, creating a strong barbarian thrust into what is now Belgium in *c.*259, passing through Raetia into north Italy in the 260s (cf. note 5); when they gained possession of the Agri Decumates (which included the Black Forest, part of the Neckar basin and the Swabian Alps), and even penetrating into Spain, they were effectively punished by Maximian (286–345). The Alamanni were often associated with the Franks, who from the early third century formed a combination of numerous tribes just beyond the Lower Rhine. There were many Franks in the army of the usurper Postumus, but later the free Franks and Alamanni, encouraged by the weakening of the Rhine defences, invaded Gaul, taking or destroying sixty of its cities. Because of them, the Roman frontier below Vetera (Xanten) was abandoned, and its linear line replaced by scattered *castella*.

5 J.F. Drinkwater, op. cit., p. 1293. Gallienus only halted the Marcomanni by ceding them part of Upper Pannonia. The Juthungi, a Germanic (Swabian) people who often joined up with the Alamanni, crossed the

upper Danube in 259, but were twice defeated in Italy. Earlier, Valerian (whose natural base was Mediolanum [Milan]) had brought up troops from Italy to help Gallus. Postumus failed to hold off the Alamanni. Diocletian created a new military command under the *dux Raetiarum*, whose headquarters were at Augusta Vindelicorum (Augsburg).

6 F. Owen, op. cit., p. 91. The Bastarnae were the first Germanic people to appear in the Black Sea area, foreshadowing the Goths (whom ancient writers sometimes confused with the 'Scythians'). The Goths were said to have come from Scandinavia (cf. the *Getica* of Jordanes, but this has sometimes been contested. Philip defeated the Goths and the Carpi (an extensive Germanic tribe centred on Dacia), but they were still perilous. Their raids under Trebonianus Gallus are ill-reported; but he seems to have been too acquiescent. Aemilian proved unable to clear Thrace of hostile bands. The Quadi were a Germanic tribe of the Swabic group. The Jazyges eventually settled between the Rivers Danube and Tisza (Theiss). The Roxolani, who were of Sarmatian origin, shared Gothic raids into Moesia. The Sarmatians, who raided with the Goths and controlled most of Pannonia, were not Germanic but Iranian [mention must also be made of the Huns: E.A. Thompson, *The Huns*, 1948, 1957].

Treaty-like agreements were made by the Romans, but the death of Timesitheus (243) encouraged Gothic incursions. They had already shown an unwillingness to return home; and, stimulated by the death of the Roman emperor Decius at Abrittus (251), continued to attack in the 250s (when Gallus hurried back to Rome – and Gothic attacks on northern Asia Minor followed), and in the 260s. The Cimmerian Bosphorus (Crimea) formed a base for these attacks in Asia Minor, and there was a giant Gothic invasion of Greece.

The Goths were Rome's worst enemy, exerting continual pressures. They were helped by the Heruli, a relatively primitive Germanic people, who launched an invasion in 268 from several bases, and won vast prizes but from a military viewpoint were unsuccessful in the long run. See P. Heather, *The Goths*. The division of the Goths into the Visigoths and Ostrogoths dates from the end of the third century. Some of them helped the Romans against the Persian Sapor (Shapur) I (see next chapter).

7 M. Todd, *The Early Germans* (1992), pp. 58ff.

3 THE PERSIANS

1 The Sas(s)anian empire, at its greatest size, extended from Syria to India, and from Iberia to the Persian Gulf. The Persians, it has been said, did not know much about the art of war, but relied on courage. It has been suggested that they owed more to their Parthian predecessors than to the old Achaemenid Persians, whom they admired. The predecessor of Sapor I, Ardashir, captured Nisibis (Nüsaybin) and Carrhae (Altibasak) under Maximinus I, overrunning Mesopotamia, as part of the Sas(s)anian plan to restore ancient frontiers. There was no formal peace, but Sapor's defeat at R(h)esaena (Theodosiopolis, Ras-el-Ain) in 243,

preceded by the Roman recovery of Nisibis and Carrhae, created a peaceful situation (extended by the withdrawal of Gordian III), which ceased in 256 when there were renewed Persian attacks.

The idea of 'Iran' developed a concept of national identity, but Sapor aimed wider, calling himself, as stated in the text, 'King of Kings of Iran and non-Iran'. The situation of Armenia has been much discussed but it seems to have remained under Persian control when Odaenathus forced Sapor I to leave Roman territory, cf. S. Williams, *Diocletian and the Roman Recovery* (1985, 1997), p. 29.

2 D.R. Dudley, *The Romans* (1970), p. 260; cf. J. Whatmough, *Oxford Classical Dictionary*, 3rd edn. (1996), pp. 135ff. Sapor's lack of diplomacy was said to be evident in his treatment of Zenobia. See also R. Stoneman, *Palmyra and its Empire*, 1984. But he captured Antioch in 253 and 260, and his spectacular successes against Rome (taking full advantage of its weakness, and culminating in his victory of 262); cf. S. Williams, op. cit. p. 29) were celebrated on the famous rock-reliefs at Naqsh-i-Rustam (*Res Gestae Divi Saporis*). He defeated and captured the Roman emperor Valerian (originally not unsuccessful, cf. his coins, but subsequently besieged at Edessa [Urfa]), thus throwing the Roman provinces open to him. There is a cameo of Sapor I celebrating his capture of Valerian in E. Strong, *Art in Ancient Rome*, II (1929), p. 104, fig. 514. For his anti-Roman imperialism, cf. R.N. Frye, *The Heritage of Persia* (1963), pp. 246f. Galerius, after an initial setback, defeated the Persian King Narses in 297. For Armenia see M. Shahin, *The Kingdom of Armenia* (1991).

4 STRONG EMPERORS

1 For the Greek tendencies of Gallienus, cf. G.W. Bowersock, *Hellenism in Late Antiquity*, paperback (1996), and Chapter 9. Gallienus rewarded Odaenathus for his help against Sapor I of Persia and Quietus.

2 J.F. Drinkwater, *Oxford Classical Dictionary*, 3rd edn, 1996, p. 1235.

3 The coin inscribed INTERNV(N)TIVS DEORVM probably signifies an agreement with Gallienus. Postumus was succeeded by Victorinus and Tetricus, who was subjugated by Aurelian.

4 B.H. Warmington and J.F. Drinkwater, *Oxford Classical Dictionary*, 3rd edn, 1996, p. 858. Gallienus called himself RESTITVTOR ORIENTIS and PANNONIAE. There is still something of a mystery about the coin on which his head is accompanied by the inscription GALLIENAE AVGVSTAE. Was this inscription mere nastiness on the part of someone at the mint, or is it a sort of vocative (H. Mattingly and E. Sydenham, *Roman Imperial Coinage*, I, p. 101, n. 115)?

5 J.F. Drinkwater, op cit., p. 340. The origins of Claudius II Gothicus are uncertain. He probably came from Illyricum, and was born in *c*.214. His coin-portraits stress his abnegation and austere virtue. On coming to the throne he at once had to take the field against the Alamanni, who had penetrated into Italy from Raetia; fighting around Lake Benacus (Garda), he also defeated the Goths near Fanum Fortunae (Fano) and Ticinum (Pavia). Later, a number of battles were fought near Marcianopolis (Preslav).

According to some, his victory at Naissus (Niş; celebrated by himself as VICTORIA GOTHIC) has been exaggerated; and certainly Claudius II Gothicus failed to destroy the Goths. But they lost much booty to him, and were checked by him, so that he could call himself 'Gothicus Maximus'. They were helped by the Heruli, who launched an expedition through the Hellespont (Dardanelles). There was an important battle near Ariminum (Rimini).

6 J.F. Drinkwater, op. cit., p. 219. Aurelian was stern, savage and bloodthirsty. In spite of evacuating Dacia (which was already effectively occupied by the Visigoths, or at least underwent a symbiotic process), Aurelian called himself DACICVS MAXIMVS: he created new provinces south of the Danube, and minted at Serdica (Sofia). Aurelian also succeeded in crushing the Franks, and celebrated a massive triumph, describing himself, with some justification, as RESTITVTOR ORBIS, ORIENTIS and SAECVLI. For Dacia, cf. V. Parvan, *Dacia* (1928); there is also an exhibition on the area at Florence in 1997 (Palazzo Strozzi). Cf. H. Mattingly, *Cambridge Ancient History*, vol. XII (1956), p. 300.

7 J.F. Drinkwater, *Oxford Classical Dictionary*, 3rd edn (1996), p. 163.

8 A.H.M. Jones, ibid., pp. 1145ff. Aurelian, rather vaguely, called himself PARTHICVS MAXIMVS. The coins of Vaballathus, the son of Odaenathus and Zenobia, with and without Aurelian, remain somewhat controversial: were they minted with, or without, the consent of the imperial Roman government? He received none of the titles of his father except that of King of Palmyra. Zenobia invaded Egypt and most of Asia Minor, up to the Hellespont; she was said to have refused Aurelian's terms twice before she was captured. See also V. Schaefer, *Septimia Zenobia Sebaste* (1992).

9 H. Mattingly, *Cambridge Ancient History*, vol. XII (1956), p. 300.

10 D.R. Dudley, *The Romans* (1970, pp. 36ff.

11 J.B. Ward-Perkins in A. Boethius and J.B. Ward-Perkins, *Etruscan and Roman Architecture* (1970), pp. 406ff.

12 E. Strong, *Art in Ancient Rome*, vol. II (1929), pp. 169f.

13 J.B. Ward-Perkins, op. cit., pp. 497ff.

14 J.F. Drinkwater, op. cit., p. 1471. Tacitus probably came from the Danube area – and his claim to have been related to the historian of the same name may well be erroneous. He celebrated his 'victory' over the Goths (which was accompanied by a defeat) with coins inscribed VICTORIA GOTH., and GOTHICVS MAXIMVS. He was killed by his troops (or by disease). His successor Florian (allegedly his brother) celebrated VICTORIA PERPETVA and SECVRITAS SAECVLI, and called himself PACATOR ORBIS. But his reign was very brief, because he failed to cope with a more experienced rival, Probus.

15 J.F. Drinkwater, op. cit., p. 1250. The mother of Probus was nobler than his father. Probus is credited with the over-optimistic remark that armies would shortly become unnecessary. For unspecified successes, he took the title PERSICVS MAXIMVS. The Isaurians were a band of people of central (southern) Asia Minor, who later provided the east with emperors.

16 H. Mattingly and B.H. Warmington, *Oxford Classical Dictionary*, 2nd edn (1970), p. 579. The Franks had to face a huge Roman army, which Probus took with him because Gaul was in such turmoil and had suffered such widespread destruction. His deliverance of the country was the most important event of his largely successful reign. His Triumph in Rome, however, used up much of the gold he had acquired.

17 J.F. Dobson, *Oxford Classical Dictionary*, 3rd edn (1996), p. 297.

18 Cf. H. Mattingly, ibid., 2nd edn (1970), p. 310. Caras' war against Persia has been described as an ambitious gamble, S. Williams, *Diocletian and the Roman Rocovery*, p. 33. How he died is uncertain, ibid., pp. 33ff. Numerian abandoned all idea of conquests.

5 THE ARMY RECONSTITUTED

1 M. Grant, *The Climax of Rome* (1968), pp. 36ff. Osrhoene (capital Edessa) was in north-western Mesopotamia. Its population was mainly Aramean.

2 M. Grant *The Army of the Caesars* (1974), p. 275. Gallienus extended Valerian's policy of celebrating military victory (VICT. GERMA-NICA). He called himself Restorer of the Gauls, and, indeed, of the human race, to which he claimed to have brought peace and security. In addition, moreover, to the coins mentioned in the text, he celebrated the Faith and Concord of the Army (as well as the Faith of the Praetorians). He himself as stated, inaugurated a new concept of defence in depth: the Augustan system, not plagued with so many frontier wars, had not envisaged the establishment of any strategic reserve. However, as has been suggested above, it is possible to interpret Gallienus's substitution of senators by knights as legionary commanders (see Chapter 4) as due, in part at least, to the desire to stave off usurpers. Nevertheless, the term 'militarisation', applied to the empire since the time of Severus, has to be used with care, although Gallienus did commemorate, on coins, the legions which had furnished units for his army. The rank of the legionary was at its highest at this time; but the Moorish, Dalmatian and Osrhoenian mounted auxiliaries were also strong.

3 Ibid., pp. 276ff.

4 M. Grant, *Constantine* (1995), p. 225.

6 DIOCLETIAN

1 R.P. Davis, *Oxford Classical Dictionary*, 3rd edn (1996), p. 470; cf. M. Platnauer, *The Age of Diocletian: A Symposium* (1933); S. Williams, *Diocletian and the Roman Recovery* (1985, 1997); for his qualities, *ibid.*, p. 27. Was he, by origin, a freedman or a slave?

2 A. Ferrill in M. Grant and R. Kitzinger (eds), *Civilisation of the Ancient Mediterranean*, vol. I (1988), p. 78. For the intense system of taxation see S. Williams, op cit., p. 32; many were forced, because of it, to leave their land.

3 R.A.G. Carson, *Principal Coins of the Romans*, vol. I (1978), p. 178. Diocletian was of humble origin. He was perhaps born at Spalatum (Split), where a palace was built for him after his abdication. His brutal energy was noteworthy. Lactantius observed that he started a new era. Not only did he reform the army, but he also reorganised the Roman empire into more numerous provinces, organised in thirteen dioceses. 'Diocletian's administrative measures did much to prolong the unity of the empire for another century' (H. Mattingly and B.H. Warmington, *Oxford Classical Dictionary*, op. cit., p. 347). Yet his return to a natural economy was accompanied by a sacrifice of the interests of the individual, under a régime of state absolutism. For Diocletian's keen pagan religion, see Chapter 8.

4 M. Grant, *The Roman Emperors* (1985), pp. 203ff. Maximian, a fanatical man, had to deal with a new German breakthrough. He also employed Constantius to destroy Allectus (296), who had succeeded Carausius in 293 as emperor (usurper) in Britain and northern Gaul; he kept the Caledonians out of northern Britain (see P.J. Casey, *Carausius and Allectus* (1994)). Galerius fought the Carpi in Roumania four times, and was defeated by the Persians (296), but then defeated them heavily and got back Armenia, which the Persians had seized (Tiridates III ruled from 287).

The Tetrarchy were an effective team, who organised military recovery, though financial straitness was exacerbated. It came to an end, basically, because of the unprecedented abdication in 305 of Diocletian, who had been unquestionably the master. The Second Tetrarchy, which followed this abdication, did not last; it remained for Constantine to reunite the empire. Whether Diocletian abdicated because of ill-health, or for another reason, has been much discussed, see C. Howgego, op. cit.

5 J.B. Ward-Perkins in A. Boethius and J.B. Ward-Perkins, *Etruscan and Roman Architecture* (1970), pp. 517f., 522, 536.

6 There is an Arch of Galerius at Thessalonica (Salonica), and a number of columns belonging to the palace of Maximian survive at Mediolanum (Milan).

> The palace which Diocletian built at Antioch [Antakya] . . . on the island opposite the Hellenistic city – lies deep . . . beneath the silt of the Orontes [River Nahr-el-Asi], but [is] described by the fourth-century writer Libanius. . . . Libanius adds that at the far side the wall was crowned by a colonnade offering a view over the river and the suburbs beyond. Adjoining it was a hippodrome. The plan was certainly not a near rectangle, and the palace did not occupy the whole of the fortified enclosure.
> (J.B. Ward-Perkins, op. cit., pp. 527ff).

7 D.R. Dudley, *The Romans* (1976), p. 703.

8 M.R. Scherer, *Marvels of Ancient Rome* (1955, 1956), p. 98; E. Strong, *Art in Ancient Rome*, vol. II (1929), pp. 71f. As for Diocletian himself, he only came to Rome once.

7 COINAGE AND FINANCE

1 According to C.V. Sutherland, *Roman Coins* (1974), p. 98:

> The weight of the *aureus*, the anchor of the Roman monetary system, fell progressively: by the time of Gallienus, it scarcely adhered to any standard of weight at all, it was often accompanied by pieces of one-third, and even the fineness of gold was variable. . . . Silver, too, was grievously affected. . . . The *antoninianus* itself [if this is what it was called; its name is uncertain] was progressively debased until, by *c.*270, its silver content was nominal. *Aes* [bronze], in its turn, also suffered.
> . . . Although we lack any contemporary analysis of monetary history (or even price-changes) of those times the lesson is clear. Confidence in the coinage was collapsing . . . *Aes* had thrust upon it an even less than purely token role which resulted in the production of vast numbers of almost pure copper *antoniniani*.

See also J. Williams (ed.) *Money: A History* (1997), C. Howgego, *Ancient History from Coins* (1995).
2 Aurelian issued new and improved silver-washed coins, and his *aurei* (gold) were all of the right weight. He did not attempt what might well be described as impossible, so his arrangements were somewhat makeshift. The mint of Rome revolted, under Felicissimus. Prices continued to rise. Cf. C. Howgego, op. cit.
3 M. Grant, *The Roman Emperors* (1985), pp. 264ff.
4 M. Grant, *Roman Imperial Money* (1954), pp. 252, 297.
5 H. Mattingly, *Roman Coins* (1960, 1928), p. 212.
6 M. Grant, *The Emperor Constantine* (1993), p. 225.
7 C.H.V. Sutherland, *Roman Coins* (1974), pp. 225ff.

8 STATE RELIGION

1 For example, the tendency was turned to good advantage by the State: the series of coins with the heads of long deified emperors, usually attributed to Trajanus Decius, but possibly issued by Trebonianus Gallus.
2 M. Grant *The Climax of Rome* (1968), pp. 175ff., 283. Aurelian honoured Sol Invictus, and saw himself as his vice regent. This remained the chief imperial cult until Christianity. But Jupiter was not neglected: Diocletian called himself 'Jovius', and Maximian 'Herculius'. An effort was also made – as numerous coins show – to exalt the GENIVS POPVLI ROMANI.
3 M.R. Scherer, *Marvels of Ancient Rome* (1955, 1956), pp. 108ff. For the Sun cult, especially at the time of Gallienus, see also C. Minelli, *Rendiconti del Istituto Lombardo, Classe di Lettere ecc.*, 130, 1996, pp. 25f.
4 H. Mattingly, *Cambridge Ancient History*, vol. XII (1956), p. 309.
5 J.B. Ward-Perkins in A. Boethius and J.B. Ward-Perkins, *Etruscan and Roman Architecture* (1970), p. 498.

6 M. Grant, *The Climax of Rome* (1968), pp. 178ff., 273.
7 Ibid., pp. 180ff.
8 Ibid., pp. 180ff. It has lately been argued that much of the Arch of
   Constantine is of considerably earlier date.
9 M. Grant, *Constantine the Great* (1993), pp. 221ff., 50. For the peculiarity
   of Constantine's Christianity cf. H. Pohlsander, *The Emperor Constantine*
   (1996), pp. 86f., quoting other scholars. See also P. Brown, *Authority and
   the Sacred: Aspects of the Christianisation of the Roman World* (1997). Christianity had been persecuted by Diocletian, who was nevertheless personally, it has been asserted, averse to bloodshed. Constantine's
   adherence to the faith, unlike that of many others (E. Strong, *Art
   in Ancient Rome*, vol. III [1929], p. 169), was partly conditioned by
   Sun-worship (e.g. 25 December was the birthday of the Sun-god).
   But the pagan, Julian, later, who was well disposed to Syrians, was
   devoted to the Sun. On Mithraism see R. Gordon, *Image and Value
   in the Graeco-Roman World: Studies in Mithraism and Religious Art*
   (1996).

9 PHILOSOPHY AND PERSONAL RELIGION

1 E.R. Dodds and J.M. Dillon, *Oxford Classical Dictionary*, 3rd edn (1996),
   pp. 1198ff.
2 M. Grant, *The Climax of Rome* (1968), pp. 150ff., 140ff. Plotinus has
   been described as the most powerful philosophical mind between
   Aristotle and Descartes. Nevertheless, his school at Rome did not
   survive his death; the *Enneads* are posthumous, dateable to *c*.300–
   303. But his earlier approach to Gallienus was not unreasonable for
   that emperor, as already stated, had Hellenistic interests. See J.M.
   Narbonne, *La métaphysique de Plotin* (1996). A.H. Armstrong, who
   studied Plotinus, died in 1997.
3 Ibid., pp. 200ff; cf. p. 203. Mani was believed to have been born in
   c.177 and to have died in 216. He was a friend of Sapor I, but
   Mazdaean (Sun) influence under a later king, Bahram I, led to his
   death. Mani encouraged asceticism, and found room for Jesus.
4 M. Grant *Constantine the Great* (1993), p. 166. For Gnosticism, see
   M. Seymour-Smith, *Gnosticism: The Role of Inner Knowledge* (1996).
5 M. Grant, *The Climax of Rome* (1968), pp. 202ff.

10 HELIODORUS AND THE *AETHIOPICA*

1 N. Holzberg, *The Ancient Novel* (1995, 1986), pp. 33ff. The question of
   who read novels (or romances, as some prefer to call them), still stands.
   But undoubtedly many people did.
2 M. Grant, *Greeks and Romans: A Social History* (1992), p. 35; G. Anderson,
   Ancient Fiction (1984), pp. 1ff., 220. Ovid, *Ars Amatoria*, vol. III, had
   already advised his readers to take an interest in current literature.
3 P.E. Easterling and B.M.W. Knox (eds), *The Cambridge History of Classical
   Literature, I, Greek Literature* (1985), pp. 694f. Heliodorus's date is
   uncertain: perhaps he wrote in *c*.220–250 – and no novelist seems to

have come after him. He was the most ambitious of seven novelists influenced by the Second Sophistic, but he tangles many threads, and writes – with pompous pedantry as well as literary point – a very artificial Greek, overloaded with participles. He is keen on biography and historiography (though often not very accurate): he innovates by making his hero and heroine spend the rest of their lives in a far-off land – although he himself, apparently, went to Rome. He is an expert of tension between what ought to happen, and what in fact does. He wants to stimulate readers, not to deter them. His great strength is narrative, laced with wonderful adventures.

4 G. Giangrande, *Encyclopaedia Britannica* (1971 edn), vol. XI, p. 316. Heliodorus was a devout pagan, and the whole work is written under the sign of the (Emesan) Sun-god. Heliodorus is deeply interested in religious mysticism, as well as in sacerdotal solemnities. His work has a somewhat oriental look; but his attitudes to 'race' need reconsidering. Underdowne's translation of 1507 was reprinted with an introduction by G. Sainsbury (Abbey Classics 23).

5 M. Grant, *The Climax of Rome* (1968), p. 129.

6 E.L. Bowie, *Oxford Classical Dictionary*, 3rd edn (1996), pp. 676, 1051.

7 G. Giangrande, ibid., 2nd edn (1970), pp. 493ff.

APPENDIX

1 Cleisthenes, of the family of the Alcmaeonidae, was elected archon for 508–507. He was generally regarded as the creator of the Athenian democracy, although his constitution sometimes seemed too aristocratic to warrant this description.

2 The Ionian Revolt was triggered off by Aristagoras of Miletus (Balat), who brought about a general expulsion of 'tyrants' from the Ionian cities of western Asia Minor (499).

3 The Persian Wars also strengthened the Greek belief in the benignity and power of their gods, over whom Zeus (called Jupiter by the Romans) presided.

4 'Delian League' is the modern name given to the great alliance against the Persians. At the allies' request, Athens accepted the leadership. At the outset, policy was determined at meetings on the sacred island of Delos, a traditional Ionian festival centre, at which every member had an equal vote, although Athens reversed this.

5 This Persian intervention in the Pelopennesian War was a very important factor which is not always sufficiently recognised by western chauvinists. It came about because the Spartan general and statesman Lysander, appointed admiral for 408–407, gained the friendship and support of the Persian prince Cyrus. Cf. A. Powell, *Athens and Sparta* (1988).

6 For this period see M. Grant, *From Alexander to Cleopatra* (1982) (reprinted as *The Hellenistic Greeks*, 1990).

7 The Parthians were Rome's only unified neighbours and enemies, based on Iran (Persia) and eastern Mesopotamia (Iraq). But they were not as effectively centralised as the Persians who followed them.

8 For Caesar, cf. M. Grant, *Julius Caesar* (1969).
9 Cf. M. Grant, *The Twelve Caesars* (1975).
10 Cf. M. Grant, *The Severans* (1996).
11 Cf. M. Grant, *The Roman Emperors* (1985), pp. 137ff.
12 Cf. M. Grant, *The Emperor Constantine* (1993).
13 Cf. M. Grant, *The Fall of the Roman Empire* (1976).
14 W. Warde-Fowler, *Rome* (1912, 1967), p. 112.
15 G. Highet, *The Classical Tradition* (1949, 1967), pp. 1ff.
16 R.E.M. Wheeler, *Swan's Hellenic Cruise Handbook* (1962, 1982), p. 48.
17 B. Knox, *Essays Ancient and Modern* (1992), p. 161. In a thousand different ways the Greeks and the Romans are indestructibly woven into our own existence. Every new generation sees its own problems reflected in Greece and Rome: without knowledge of what they did, our own experience, it has been said, is built on sand; so the continual re-excavation of our classical past is essential. Cf. also C.M. Bowra, *A Classical Education: Presidential Address to the Classical Association* (1945), R.R. Bolgar, *The Classical Heritage and its Beneficiaries* (5th impression, 1977), H. Lloyd-Jones, *Classical Survivals* (1982). T.S. Eliot observed that the bloodstream of European literature is Latin and Greek. Without them, our world would be thinner, more fragmentary and more materialistic. Yet, inevitably, every individual's approach and reaction to the classical era has to be personal. See J.P. Hallett and T. van Nortwick (eds), *Compromising Traditions: The Personal Voice in Classical Scholarship* (1996). Classical inspirations were analysed at a congress at Madingly Hall, Cambridge, in July 1996, and I lectured on the subject at Nottingham University in April 1998. But sight should not be lost of the remarkable period covered by this book.
18 M. Grant, *Roman Literature* (1954), pp. 7, 272ff., and *A Short History of Classical Civilisation* (1991), p. 1. 'Humanism is closely linked with the Greco-Roman tradition, and the noblest ideal of the Romans, in particular, was *humanitas*, a blend of culture and kindness', cf. L.P. Wilkinson, *Encyclopaedia Britannica* (1970 edn), vol. XIII, pp. 780f., M. Grant, *The Roman Experience* (1975), p. 22, see p. 172. On the complicated question of Rome's indebtedness to Greece, see A. Wardman, *Rome's Debt to Greece* (1996); see A. Raubitschek, *The School of Hellas* (1991). See also P. Green, *Classical Bearings* (1989), G.S. Meltzer, *The Humanities: Ancient and Postmodern Classical Outlook* (1996), pp. 81ff.
19 J. Percival, in B.R. Rees (ed.), *Classics* (1970), pp. 55ff. 'What a luxury!' Lady Thatcher is believed to have said about history. She would feel the same about the period of temporary collapse described in this book.
20 C.W. Baty, *Encyclopaedia Britannica* (1970 edn), vol. V, p. 875. What Dean Gaisford actually said was: 'Nor can I do better, in conclusion, than impress upon you the study of Greek literature, which not only elevates above the vulgar herd, but leads not infrequently to positions of considerable emolument.' For details, including the inevitable boomerang, see R.M. Ogilvie, *A History of the Influence of the Classics on English Life, 1600-1918* (1964), and for the problems raised by Greeks, Joint Association of Classical Teachers, *An Independent Study*

Guide to Reading Greek (1995), and Carol Handley (Course Director), *General Prospectus for Reading Classical Greek* (1996); cf. L. Kellett, *General Prospectus for Reading Latin* (1996). The number of students taking A-level Latin and Greek has gone down from 3,117 + 583 in 1975 to 1,625 + 283 in 1995. But P. Jones, *The Times*, 13 July 1996, although admitting the decline, claims that 'Latin is ripe for revival.' And there has been a lot of recent interest in Roman Britain: see e.g. P. Salway, *The Oxford Illustrated History of Roman Britain*. There is also a book (ed., W. Haase and M. Reinhold), entitled *The Classical Tradition and the American* (vol. I, Part 1). The temporary decline of the Roman empire, described in this book, tends to make people forget about the lasting Greco-Roman tradition.

21 M. Grant, *Readings in the Classical Historians* (1992), pp. 22ff. 'Lessons and warnings' from history are nowadays dismissed as old-fashioned – perhaps prematurely? Ancient historians were supposed to give pleasure: that is one reason why they were sometimes inaccurate. But inaccuracy persisted.

> Who can claim that he or she has the slightest idea of what is really happening today? Name any country that is undergoing a crisis, anywhere. Are we really able to suppose that we can understand what is happening there? Of course not. There are many conflicting accounts, and some or all of them are untrue. . . . Can we trust anyone to tell us, reliably, what is going on? We cannot. If that is the case today, how much more so is it the case with events that happened many centuries ago?
>
> (ibid., p. 126)

22 J.C. Stobart, *The Grandeur That Was Rome* (1912), p. 296.
23 R.E.M. Wheeler, *Swan's Hellenic Cruises* (1952, 1982), p. 48.
24 The Parthenon and Erechtheum (on which see below) are respectively of the Doric and Ionic architectural Orders. These are defined as follows (S. Woodford, *The Cambridge Introduction to Art: Greece and Rome* [1982], p. 25):

> The Doric Order was strong, simple and massive. . . . The capitals surmounting the shafts were simple, cushion-like dwellings topped by an undecorated, square *abacus*, which supported a plain undivided architecture. This is turn supported the frieze. . . . The Ionic Order was more delicate and ornate. . . . Ionic capitals curve over to the right and left to end in volutes.

(The other important Order, much used in Hellenistic and Roman times, was the Corinthian, which displayed bell-shaped capitals with rows of acanthus leaves.) For modern trends in archaeology, cf. P. Reilly and S. Rahtz (eds), *Archaeology and the Information Age* (1992). The 'new archaeology', it is said, 'will save time and money'. It has been particularly esteemed in the United States. But cf. R. Layton (ed.), *Who Needs the Past?*, paperback (1995). It has been remarked that 'computer archaeology is doing for the strategy of archaeology what metal detectors have done for its tactics'. Remote-sensing magnetometers are linked to computers. The new science is called geophysical technology. But archaeology has already been developing rapidly in recent years: witness work on the Anastasian Wall in Thrace, M. Grant, *From Rome to Byzantium* (1998; the work of James Crow).

25 S. Perowne, *The End of the Roman World* (1966), p. 137.

26 B.F. Rhodes, *Architecture and Meaning in the Athenian Acropolis* (1995).

27 M. Grant, *The Cities of Vesuvius* (1971): and review in *The Times* 2 September 1997 of R. Lings, *The Insula of the Menander at Pompeii*, vol. I, *The Structures* (1997); there have also been many other publications.

28 M. Grant, *The Emperor Constantine* (1993), P1.2. Cf. also H.P. L'Orange, *Studien zur Geschichte der spätantiken Porträts* (1993). Reference should also be made to the development of non-imperial portrait busts, for example at Palmyra (Tadmor), M. Grant, *Art in the Roman Empire* (1995). Portraiture shows how intensely interested the Romans were in individuality.

29 A metope is the panel (plain or sculptured) between the triglyphs (projecting members divided into three strips by two vertical grooves) of a Doric entablature (the horizontal superstructure carried by a colonnade).

30 *Sculpture from the Parthenon and Other Greek Temples* (British Museum), p. 4. Cf. B. Cook, *The Elgin Marbles* (1984), pp. 18f., 24, 34; cf. p. 6. The Ara Pacis at Rome reveals strong Greek influence.

31 M. Grant, *Art in the Roman Empire* (1995), p. 23 and figs 5, 6; and P. MacKendrick, *The Dacian Stones Speak* (1975), pp. 95, 97, 105; cf. L. Rossi, *Trajan's Column and the Dacian Wars* (1971). Reference should also be made to the portrait-sculpture on gems, e.g. the *Gemma Augustea*, M. Grant, op. cit., pp. 112ff., and to round stone table-tops (altars), with the Christogram, and to Coptic stone reliefs (e.g. of a Nereid, with fish), and to fragments of plates, and to decorated oil lamps from Syria, R. Temple (ed.), *Early Christian and Byzantine Art* (1990), pp. 62ff., 73, 76, 79–86. For the cameo of Sapor I, see above, Chapter 3; cf. also J. Ogden, *Ancient Jewellery* (1992), L. Barbocci, *Antike Gläser* (1996).

32 M. Grant, op. cit., pp. 91ff., quoting S. Rozenberg, *Enchanted Landscapes: Wall-Paintings from the Roman Empire* (1994), pp. 9, 12ff; cf. p. 162, n. 11.

33 S. Rozenberg, op. cit., p. 93.

34 Ibid., pp. 95f. Most of the paintings (which are now exhibited in an international exhibition) came from the cemeteries of Moeris (the Fayum Oasis), 60 miles south of Cairo, where a lake is linked by a canal to the River Nile. There are labels, however, which indicate that certain dead people from Philadelphia (Darb Gerze), in the north-eastern Fayum, were buried beside the Nile itself. The Detroit painting of a man was at Antinoupolis (Sheikh Ibada), and is of the later first century AD. For textiles, cf. R. Temple (ed.), *Early Christian and Byzantine Art* (1990), pp. 25ff., 30–33.

35 M. Grant, *Roman History from Coins* (1958), pp. 1188.

SOURCES

1 GREEK

ACHILLES TATIUS of Alexandria. Second-century AD. Novelist, author of *The Adventures of Leucippe and Clitophon.*

AESCHYLUS of Eleusis, 525/4–456 BC. Tragic dramatist, author of *Seven Against Thebes, Suppliants, Prometheus Bound, Persians, Oresteia (Agamemnon, Choephoroe, Eumenides).*

ARISTOPHANES of Athens, 487–485/shortly before 385 BC. Dramatist of Old Comedy, author of *Archarnians, Knights, Clouds, Wasps, Peace, Birds, Lysistrata, Thesmophoriazusae, Frogs, Ecclesiazusae, Plutus.*

ARISTOTLE of Stagirus, 384–322 BC. Philosopher and scientist.

BASIL of Caesarea (Cappodocia, Kayseri) c.AD 330–379. Christian writer.

DEMOSTHENES of Athens, 384–322 BC. Orator and statesman.

DIO CASSIUS (Cassius Dio Cocceianus) of Nicaea (Bithynia; Iznik). Late second and early third century AD. Historian.

EUNAPIUS of Sardes (Sart) in Lydia, Asia Minor, c.AD 345–420. Philosopher (Sophist).

EURIPIDES of Phlya (Attica), c.485/480–c.406 BC. Tragic dramatist, author of *Alcestis, Medea, Hippolytus, Andromache, Hecuba, Troades, Phoenissae, Orestes, Bacchae, Rhesus(?), Helen, Electra, Heracleidae, Heracles, Suppliants, Iphigenia in Aulis, Iphigenia in Tauris, Ion, Cyclops.*

GALEN of Pergamum (Bergama), AD 129–?199. Medical writer and monotheistic philosopher.

HELIODORUS, third century AD. Novelist, author of *Aethiopica.*

HERODOTUS of Halicarnassus (Caria; Bodrum), 480–425 BC. Historian.

HESIOD of Cyme (Aeolis) and Ascra (Boeotia), eighth century BC. Epic poet.

HOMER, probably born in Chios and worked at Smyrna (Izmir), eighth century BC. Epic poet, reputed author of *Iliad* and *Odyssey.*

JOHN CHRYSOSTOM, c.AD 354–407. Educated at Antioch, Bishop of Constantinople. Christian writer.

JULIAN THE APOSTATE. Emperor, AD 361–363, author of *Misopogon* and *Caesares* and many letters.

LIBANIUS, AD 314–c.393. Author of speeches and letters.

LONGUS, probably from Lesbos, perhaps late second century and early third century AD. Novelist, author of *Daphnis and Chloe.*

LUCIAN of Samosata (Samsat in Syria). Born *c.*120 AD. Writer on many subjects.

MARCUS AURELIUS, Emperor AD 161–180. Author of *Meditations*.

MENANDER of Athens, 342/1–293/89 BC. Dramatist of New Comedy. Of his many plays, one, the *Dyskolos*, has survived complete.

PAUSANIAS of Lydia(?), second century AD. Traveller and geographer.

PINDAR of Cynoscephalae (Boeotia), *c.*518–*c.*438 BC. Lyric poet.

PLATO of Athens, *c.*429–347 BC. Outstanding philosopher.

PLOTINUS of Lycopolis, in Egypt, AD 205–269/70. Philosopher.

PLUTARCH (Lucius Messius Plutarchus) of Chaeronea (Boeotia), before AD 50–after 120. Philosopher and biographer.

PTOLEMY (Claudius Ptolemaeus), first half of second century AD. Astronomer, mathematician, geographer.

PYTHAGORAS of Samos, sixth century BC. Philosopher, man of religion and mathematician.

SAPPHO of Eresus and Mytilene (Lesbos). Born *c.*612 BC. Lyric poet.

SUDA Lexicon. End of tenth century AD.

THEOCRITUS of Syracuse (Sicily), *c.*300–*c.*260(?) BC. Pastoral poet.

THUCYDIDES of Athens, *c.*460/455–*c.* 400 BC. Historian.

2 LATIN

APULEIUS of Madaurus (Mdaurouch in Algeria). Born *c.*AD 123. Novelist, writer of *Metamorphoses (Golden Ass)*.

AUGUSTINE, St (Aurelius Augustinus) of Thagaste (Souk Ahras in Algeria), AD 354–430. Christian writer of *Confessions* (*c.*397–400), *On the City of God* (413–426), etc.

AUGUSTUS (Gaius Octavius), 63 BC–AD 14. First Roman Emperor. Author of *Res Gestae Monumentum Ancyranum*).

CAESAR (Gaius Julius), 100–44 BC. Dictator, author of *Gallic War* (7 books), *Civil War* (3 books).

CATULLUS (Gaius Valerius). Born Verona, *c.*84–54(?) BC. Lyric poet.

CICERO (Marcus Tullius). Born at Arpinum (Arpino), 106–43 BC. Orator, writer on many subjects, letter writer.

HISTORIA AUGUSTA (Scriptores Historiae Augustae). Collection of biographies of Romans from AD 117 to 284.

HORACE (Quintus Horatius Flaccus). Born at Venusia (Venosa), 65–8 BC. Poet.

JEROME, St (Eusebius Hieronymus). Born at Stridon (Dalmatia), *c.*338–420 AD. Christian writer.

LACTANTIUS (Lucius Caelius(?) Firmianus). From North Africa, *c.*AD 240–320. Christian apologist.

LIVY (Titus Livius). Born at Patavium (Padua), 64/59 BC–AD 12/17. Historian.

LUCRETIUS (Titus Lucretius Carus), *c.*94–55 BC. Philosophical poet.

OVID (Publius Ovidius Naso) of Sulmo (Sulmona). 43 BC–18 AD. Poet in hexameters and especially elegiacs.

PETRONIUS (Arbiter). First century AD. Novelist, author of *Satyricon*.

PLAUTUS (Titus Maccius) of Sarsina (Umbria). Early second century BC. Comic dramatist.

PROPERTIUS (Sextus) as Asisium (Assisi). Born 54/47 BC. Elegiac poet.

SALLUST (Gaius Sallustius Crispin) of Amiternum (Vittorino) *c*.86–35 BC. Historian.

SUETONIUS (Gaius Suetonius Tranquillus), of Pisaurum (Pesaro)(?). Born *c*.AD 69. Biographer.

TACITUS (Cornelius), *c*.AD 56–117(?). Historian and biographer, etc., author of *Agricola, Germania, Histories* and *Annals.*

TERENCE (Publius Terentius Afer), of North Africa. ?195–159 BC. Comic dramatist.

TIBULLUS (Albinus). Born 55/48 BC. Poet.

VIRGIL (Publius Vergilius Maro). Born at Andes (near Mantua), 70–19 BC. Poet, author of *Eclogues, Georgics* and *Aeneid.*

BIBLIOGRAPHY

Alföldi, A. *Cambridge Ancient History*, 1956.

Alföldi, A. *Geschichte der Weltkrise des dritten Jahrhunderts*, 1967.

Anderson, G. *Ancient Fiction*, 1984.

Anderson, J.C. *Roman Architecture and Society*, 1997.

Bandinelli, R.B. *The Late Empire: Roman Art AD 200–400*, 1995.

Barbocci, L. *Antike Gläser*, 1996.

Bastien, P. *Le buste monetaire des empereurs romains*, 3 vols, 1993.

Baty, C.W. *Encyclopaedia Britannica*, vol. V, 1970.

Bolgar, R.R. *The Classical Heritage and its Beneficiaries*, fifth impression, 1977.

Bowersock, G.W. *Hellenism in Late Antiquity*, 1996.

Bowra, C.M. *A Classical Education: Presidential Address to the Classical Association*, 1945.

Brauer, G.C. *The Age of the Soldier–Emperors: Imperial Rome AD 244–284*, 1978.

British Museum, *Sculpture from the Parthenon and Other Greek Temples*.

Brower, G.C. *The Decadent Emperors: Power and Depravity in Third Century Rome*, 1995.

Brown, P. *Authority and the Sacred: Aspects of the Christianisation of the Roman World*, 1997.

Carson, R.A.G. *Principal Coins of the Romans*, vol. I, 1978.

Casey, P.J. *Allectus*, 1994.

Claster, J.N. *The Medieval Experience: AD 300–400*, 1982.

Cook, B. *The Elgin Marbles*, 1984.

Coppola, A. *Archeologhia e propaganda*, 1996.

Cutler, A. *Late Antique and Byzantine Ivory Carving*, 1998.

Convegno: Mantua, Cultura Latina Pagana: Fra Terzo e quinto secodo dopo Cristo, Mantua, 1995.

Davis, R.P. *Oxford Classical Dictionary*, third edition, 1996.

Dobson, J.F. *Oxford Classical Dictionary*, third edition, 1996.

Dudley, D.R. *The Romans*, 1970.

Easterling, P.E. and Knox, B.M.W. (eds) *The Cambridge History of Classical Literature*, vol. I, *Greek Literature*, 1985.

Ferrill, A. in M. Grant and R. Kitzinger (eds) *Civilisation of the Ancient Mediterranean*, vol. I, 1988.

Forquet de Dorna, C. *Les Césars Africains et Syriens et l'anarchie militaire*, 1908, 1970.

Frye, R.N. *The Heritage of Persia*, 1963.

Giangrande, G. *Encyclopaedia Britannica*, vol. XI, 1971.

Gibbon, E. *The Decline and Fall of the Roman Empire*, 1776–88. [There was an Everyman edition in 1993, and in 1996 there was a Penguin Classic and Library of America edition with an introduction by David Womersley. Also the Readers' Subscription and Folio Society Edition, 1997.]

Gordon, R. *Image and Value in the Graeco-Roman World: Studies in Mithraism and Religious Art*, 1996.

Grant, M. *Roman Imperial Money*, 1954a.

Grant, M. *Roman Literature*, 1954b.

Grant, M. *Roman History from Coins*, 1958.

Grant, M. *The Climax of Rome*, 1968.

Grant, M. *Julius Caesar*, 1969.

Grant, M. *The Army of the Caesars*, 1974.

Grant, M. *The Twelve Caesars*, 1975a.

Grant, M. *The Roman Experience*, 1975b.

Grant, M. *The Fall of the Roman Empire*, 1976.

Grant, M. *From Alexander to Cleopatra*, 1982.

Grant, M. *The Roman Emperors*, 1985.

Grant, M. *The Hellenistic Greeks*, 1990.

Grant, M. *A Short History of Classical Civilisation*, 1991.

Grant, M. *Greeks and Romans: A Social History*, 1992a.

Grant, M. *Readings in the Classical Historians*, 1992b.

Grant, M. *The Emperor Constantine*, 1993a.

Grant, M. *The Emperor Constantine*, 1995a.

Grant, M. *The Severans*, 1996.

Grant, M. *Art in the Roman Empire*, 1995b.

Grant, M. *From Rome to Byzantium*, 1998.

Green, P. *Classical Bearings*, 1989.

Griard, J.B. *Gordianus II – Quintillus*, 19XX.

Grubbs, E. *Law and Family in Late Antiquity*, 1995.

Haas, C. *Alexandria in Late Antiquity*, 1995.

Hallett, J.P. and Van Nortwick (eds) *Compromising Traditions: The Personal Voice in Classical Scholarship*, 1996.

Handley, C. *General Prospectus for Reading Classical Greek*, 1996.

Harl, K.W. *Coinage in the Roman Economy 300 BC to AD 700*, 1993.

Heather, P. *The Goths*, 1996.

Highet, G. *The Classical Tradition*, 1949, 1967.

Holzberg, N. *The Ancient Novel*, 1995, 1986.

Howgego, C. *Ancient History from Coins*, 1995.

Joint Association of Classical Teachers, *An Independent Study Guide to Reading Greek*, 1995.

Jones, A.H.M. *Oxford Classical Dictionary*, second edition, 1920, pp. 1145ff.

Kellett, L. *General Prospectus for Reading Latin*, 1996.

Kisa, A. *Das Glas in Attertum*, 1908, 1968.

Knox, B. *Essays Ancient and Modern*, 1992.

Layton, R. (ed.) *Who Needs the Past?*, 1995.

Lendon, J. *Empire of Honour: The Art of Government in the Roman World*, 1997.

Lieu, S.N.C. *The Emperor Julian: Panegyric and Polemic (Mamertinus and Syrus)*, 1986.

MacKendrick, P. *The Dacian Stones Speak*, 1975.

Mattingly, H. *Cambridge Ancient History*, vol. XII, 1956.

Mattingly, H. and Sydenham, E. *Roman Imperial Coinage*, vol. I 19XX.

Mattingly, H. and Warmington, B.H. *Oxford Classical Dictionary*, second edition, 1970.

Meller, R. *History of Ancient Rome*, pb edn, 1997.

Meltzer, G.S. *The Humanities: Ancient and Postmodern Classical Outlook*, 1996.

Moorhead, I. *Theodoric in Italy*, 1902, 1987.

Musset, L. *The Germanic Invasions*, 1965, 1975.

Narbonne, J.R. *La Métaphysique de Plotin*, 1996.

Ogden, J. *Ancient Jewellery*, 1992.

Ogilvie, R.M. *A History of the Influence of the Classics on English Life, 1600–1918*, 1996.

L'Orange, H.P. *Studien zur Geschichte der spätantiken Porträts*, 1993.

Owen, F. *The Germanic Peoples*, 1990.

Oxford Classical Dictionary, 2nd edn, 1974, 3rd edn, 1966.

Percival, J. in B.R. Rees (ed.) *Classics*, 1970.

Perowne, S. *The End of the Roman World*, 1996.

Platnauer, M. *The Age of Diocletian: A Symposium*, 1933.

Pohlsander, H. *The Emperor Constantine*, 1996.

Powell, A. *Athens and Sparta*, 1988.

Prostynsky, I.P. *Utraeque res publicae: The Emperor Anastasius I's Gothic Policy*, 2nd edn, 1994.

Randers-Pehrson, J.D. *Barbarians and Romans*, 1983.

Raubitschek, A. *The School of Hellas*, 1991.

Reilly, P. and Rahtz, S. (eds) *Archaeology and the Information Age*, 1992.

Rhodes, B.F. *Architecture and Meaning in the Athenian Acropolis*, 1995.

Rossi, L. *Trajan's Column and the Dacian Wars*, 1971.

Rozenberg, S. *Enchanted Landscapes: Wall Paintings from the Roman Empire*, 1994.

Salway, P. *The Oxford Illustrated History of Roman Britain*, 1993.

Schaefer, V. *Septimia Zenobia Sebaste*, 1992.

Scherer, M.R. *Marvels of Ancient Rome*, 1955, 1956.

Seymour-Smith, M. *Gnosticism: The Role of Inner Knowledge*, 1996.

Shahim, M. *The Kingdom of Armenia*, 1991.

Spivey, N. *Understanding Greek Sculpture*, 1996.

Starr, C.G. *History of the Ancient World*, 4th edn, 1991.

Stobart, J.C. *The Grandeur That Was Rome*, 1912.

Strong, E. *Art in Ancient Rome*, vol. II, 1929.

Sutherland, C.H.V. *Roman Coins*, 1974.

Temple, R. (ed.) *Early Christian and Byzantine Art*, 1990.

Thompson, E.A. *The Huns*, 1977.

Thorpe, M. *Roman Architecture*, 1985.

Todd, M. *The Early Germans*, 1992.

Warde-Fowler, W. *Rome*, 1912, 1967.

Wardman, A. *Rome's Debt to Greece*, 1996.

Ward-Perkins, J.B. in A. Boethius and J.B. Ward-Perkins, *Etruscan and Roman Architecture*, 1970.

Warmington, B.H. and Drinkwater, J.F. *Oxford Classical Dictionary*, third edition, 1996.

Webster, L. and Brown, M. (eds) *The Transformation of the Roman World.*

Whatmough, J. *Oxford Classical Dictionary*, third edition, 1996, pp. 135ff.

Wheeler, R.M. *Swan's Hellenic Cruise Handbook*, 1962, 1982.

Wilkinson, L.P. *Encyclopaedia Britannica*, vol. XIII, 1970.

Williams, J. (ed.) *Money: A History*, 1997.

Williams, S. *Diocletian and the Roman Recovery*, 1985 and 1997.

Woodford, S. *The Cambridge Introduction to Art: Greece and Rome*, 1982.

Wrebe, P.J. *Kaiser Valens und die heidnische Opposition*, 1995.

Zecchini, G. *Ricerche di storiografa Latin – tarde antiche*, 1907.

INDEX

Michael Grant is one of the world's greatest writers on ancient history. He was formerly a Fellow of Trinity College, Cambridge, Professor of Humanities at the University of Edinburgh and Vice-Chancellor of the University of Khartoum and the Queen's University of Belfast. He has published over fifty books.